Wake up Neo....

The Matrix has you

The gate is straight
Deep and wide
Break on through
To the other side

The Doors

THE BOOK OF LIFE

ASCENSION AND
THE DIVINE WORLD ORDER

By
Michael Sharp
www.michaelsharp.org

Avatar Publications
www.avatarpublication.com

Sharp, Michael, 1963-
      The book of life : ascension and the divine world
order / by Michael Sharp.
            p. cm.
      Includes index.
      ISBN-13: 978-0-9735379-0-1 (alk. paper)
      ISBN-13: 978-0-9735379-5-6 (hardcover)
      ISBN-13: 978-0-9737401-0-3 (pdf)
      ISBN-13: 978-0-9737401-1-0 (microsoft reader)
   1. Spiritual life--Miscellanea. I. Title.

   BF1999.S436 2006
   299'.93--dc22

For information on bulk purchase discounts contact
Avatar Publications at sales@avatarpublication.com

TABLE OF CONTENTS

INDEX OF FIGURES VII

INDEX OF TABLES VIII

DEDICATION.. IX

ACKNOWLEDGEMENTS...X

INTRODUCTION..11

CHAPTER ONE: THE ENERGY OF THE ASCENSION 19

    The Ascension 19

    The Universe is about Energy.............................21

    The Physical World..26

    The Yin and the Yang of It.................................32

    Conclusion...36

CHAPTER TWO: TIME, THE UNIVERSE, AND
EVERYTHING... 38

    Introduction 38

    Life, the Universe, and Everything......................40

    Living in the Moment...50

    Concurrent Lives 51

    The End of Time/The End-times.........................55

    Prophets and Prophecy 57

    Conclusion...59

CHAPTER THREE: PREVIOUS ATTEMPTS 61

    Introduction 61

    Energy Revisited – A Question of Balance.................63

    Lemuria 66

    Energy Revisited – A Question of Connection.................71

    The Body as a Manifestation Device.................72

    Atlantis 80

    Conclusion...83

CHAPTER FOUR: OUR WORLD 85

    Introduction 85

    Energy Revisited – Entropy and Darkness.................86

    The Original Spin 88

    The One Law 91

    Transmuting Energy 94

    Karma and your Guide Network.........................96

    Keeping the Spin Controlled.............................99

    The Grays Return Home.................................. 105

Conclusion 111
CHAPTER FIVE: EMISSARIES OF LIGHT I........................113
    Introduction... 113
    The War of Souls 114
    Ascended Masters 118
    The Ascended Master Support Network (AMSN)....................124
    Conclusion 128
CHAPTER SIX: EMISSARIES OF LIGHT II 129
    Introduction... 129
    Scientists and Savants.. 130
    Communications Technology 136
    Additional Workers 141
    Children of a Higher Vibration.................................... 147
    Conclusion 151
CHAPTER SEVEN: YOUR ASCENSION PROCESS 153
    Introduction... 153
    Connect with Your Guides 156
    The Roller Coaster Ride of Ra.................................... 157
    Be of Service 162
    Clearing Blockages 163
    The Ultimate Goal 175
    Nutrition and the Body.. 177
    Conclusion 178
CONCLUSION 180
ABOUT MICHAEL SHARP... 187
INDEX.. 190

INDEX OF FIGURES

Figure One: The Tree of Life 25

Figure Two: The Space/Time Tube 42

Figure Three: The Physical Universe 44

Figure Four: Snake Ouroboros - The Cosmic Moment 49

Figure Five: The Space/Time Tube 52

Figure Six: Chakra System 75

Figure Seven: Merkaba and Light Body 79

Figure Eight: Caduceus 176

INDEX OF TABLES

Table One: Chakra Correspondences......................................76

Table Two: Chakras and Their Associated Fears.......................... 170

Table Three: Expression of Energy...................................... 173

DEDICATION

For Gina, daughter of ISIS – a powerful and gentle soul of great beauty.

For Niko whose bravery, courage, love, and sacrifice makes him truly one of the exalted ones. He is to be honored. He will be honored.

For Vayda who has chosen a difficult path of healing but who has already progressed far on that path.

For Tristan. May his light and the light of all crystal children raise this earth and its inhabitants into the New Age.

For Stephen who endured our immaturity and emerged strong and capable on the other side.

For you, the reader. You deserve nothing but love, prosperity, happiness, and peace.

Your time is now.

ACKNOWLEDGEMENTS

I would like to graciously thank Kathy and Jim who both provided invaluable editorial expertise at various stages of this project.

Thanks to OXO HALO who provided the stunning cover art and book graphics.

I would also like to thank the online community for encouraging comments that popped up like manna in my email box from time to time. Synchronistic emails often provided me with the necessary motivation to continue this project.

Very special thanks also go out to all those who provided instruction and tutorial on concepts in this book. You know who you are. Your support, encouragement, and unflinching concern that the truth be expressed at this time made the exercise of writing this book personally valuable and very memorable.

Finally, to all the Annunaki who stand behind me, and for all the those who have stood guard over the sacred passages back to divinity I say to you, our stories will soon be told and there will be much rejoicing in heaven.

INTRODUCTION

Men and people will fight ya down
When ya see Jah light.
Let me tell you if you're not wrong,
Everything is all right.
So we gonna walk - all right!
Through de roads of creation.
We the generation.
Trod through great tribulation.

Bob Marley, Exodus

Hello and welcome to the new earth!

Welcome to the most glorious event in the history of this physical universe. Indeed, welcome to the most significant event in the history of all of creation.

Although many of you may not have realized it just yet, everyone on this planet has front row seats to one of the most amazing and beautiful creative events ever initiated. All of us currently existing in, on, and around this earth are about to witness the culmination of eons of physical evolution and spiritual effort. A divine plan set in motion at the very start of this creation is reaching its glorious, divinely sanctioned, and spiritually magnificent climax. Now the entire hosts of heaven, the spiritual hierarchies, and indeed the whole of creation are poised, watching and waiting, to participate in a divine event so magnificent its description is beyond mere words. Prophecies about heaven on earth and even our greatest imaginings of paradise lost do not do justice to the scope and magnitude of this event.

Sound exciting?

It is!

And what is this event that everyone is so excited about? Well, it is known by different names in different cultures and religious doctrines. In Christian circles it is known as the creation of heaven on earth and in some eastern religions, most notably Tibetan Buddhism, it is known as the return of the kingdom of Shambhala. The Mayans knew it was coming. They ended their calendar at the approximate conclusion of it.

It is probably best described in the new age movement, where the event is known as The Ascension. The word "ascension" literally means to move upward and is a perfect term for this process because, at its root, The Ascension really is about moving up. It is about taking the whole of this physical universe and moving it back up the Ladder of Creation (or Tree of Life) to return it to the rarified and super conscious dimensional levels that exist just above and beyond our normal work-a-day consciousness.

The good news is, it is happening right now!

Although you may not have realized it yet, everything around you, from the stars and their gasses to the dirt and the dust and even your own physical body (in other words the entire physical universe) is being raised up through a quantum dimensional boundary. The physical universe is beginning a long journey back up the Tree of Life. This really is Good News because now that we have started this process, it is time to remember our role in it. It means we can remind ourselves about The Ascension and what we have done to get to this point.

That is what this book is for.

The *Book of Life* is in your hands right now so that you remember what *you* have done and where *we* are going. In the pages of this book you will be introduced to important background information that will allow you to better understand what is happening on this earth and in your own life right now.

It is important you get your bearings straight. The process that is unfolding now is a powerful process. We are all now returning to our full spiritual power. This may not sound like much to you right now but believe me, we are a lot more powerful than we have been led to believe and unless we get our bearings straight and get control of our own powerful abilities, we will run afoul of our own ability to manifest.

The bottom line is, we are becoming so powerful in our ability to create the world around us that if we don't WAKE UP right now, we may inadvertently hurt ourselves or our loved ones.

I know this sounds a bit dramatic but its true. We have to move forward. We have to wake up.

Don't worry. It is not as hard as you think and I'm here to help.

I am going to help you wake up!

I am going to help you remember who you really are!

Consider this book as "step one" on the path of awakening.

In this book, you are going to learn the basic truths about this planet and our millennial work on it. You will learn the basics about the multidimensional nature of creation[1], the nature of this particular level of the physical universe, and the importance of energy to creation. You will learn that while existing in that body of yours, you exist in the lowest physical dimension of creation. You will learn of the limitations of this low level of physicality (as well as its attractions) and the reason why ascension is such a desired and heralded event. You will learn that ascension is a physical process and quantum event that affects the physical universe that you are awake in.

It is not a difficult process to understand. As you will learn, ascension is simply the physical outcome of raising the vibratory energy

---

[1] For a more advanced treatment of the underlying truths of creation see my *Book of Light: The Nature of God, the Structure of Consciousness, and the Universe Within You.*

of physical matter. It is very much like heating up a bowl of porridge or hunk of wax. The more energy in the wax, i.e., the warmer it is, the faster the molecules are vibrating and the easier it is to shapes. This is the goal, really, heating the physical universe so it is easier to shape.

Now, getting to the point where we can ascend matter has not been an easy task. In fact, it has taken several attempts to get the wax "just right" and as you read this book, you will come to understand why it has taken so long. You will learn about our past efforts to ascend this universe and why they failed. As you learn about our past attempts (Lemuria, Atlantis), you will also learn about our current attempt (Terra) and why this attempt, the one you are currently living through, is the successful one. As you will learn, it is only now, at the "edge of time", where we, as Immortal Spirit, can claim to have cooked physicality to just the right temperature and pressure to support the new unfolding that is now occurring all around you.

As you conclude this book you will also learn about the profound implications of this event and the reason why everyone in this whole cosmos is so excited by what **you** have all achieved on this earth. As you will come to understand, it really is hard to overestimate just how important and significant your accomplishments are. The bottom line is, the successful completion of The Ascension alters our ability (as Immortal Spirit) to experience and create in the physical universe. On the one hand, raising the vibration of physical matter makes it more responsive to the creative intent of spirit. On the other hand, ascending physical reality allows us, as Immortal Spirit, to enter into physicality with the full force of our magnificent consciousness. Taken together, these two things amount to an entirely new *unfolding* of physical creation.[2]

---

[2] Although the concept of the unfolding of creation is easy to understand, nevertheless because it requires a spiritual foundation which I

So, now you know that this book is about the physical parameters and implications of The Ascension. However, the book is about more than just the physical parameters of ascension. This book is also about your place in the grand passion play that has been The Ascension drama. Questions you have about the meaning of your life (and of life in general), the reasons you incarnate on this planet, and why your life takes on the shapes and contours it does, will all be answered for you by framing them within the context of The Ascension. You will learn, perhaps to your great surprise, that your entire existence on this planet has revolved around this ascension event. That is, incarnating on this planet and participating in the spiritual work necessary to trigger ascension is the *only reason* you come here. There is no other reason. You are not here as students. You are not here to be punished. You are not a maturing spiritual entity. You are not engaged (heaven forbid!) in a struggle between good and evil. You are simply an energy worker, working diligently to alter the physical laws of this universe to make it a better place for your brothers and sisters.

Now, although I think most people reading this will at least be open to the truths that I am sharing with you, I still think that some of you may have difficulty with the ideas presented here. To totally eject any notion of a retributive God, to leave behind notions of spiritual tutelage, or cosmic struggles of good and evil, and to consider that one cosmic event, something we have worked towards for eons, is the single most important organizing feature of your life will be a hard pill to swallow.

I can understand your difficulty and I know why some of you may have difficulty here. It comes down to your training.

---

do not provide in this book, it is impossible to adequately define what I mean by an "unfolding" here. If you are interested, this advanced spiritual concept is discussed in *The Book of Light*. Volume one of The Book of Light is available for free from http://bookoflight.michaelsharp.org/

It is because of your socialization.

It is because some people have told you an organized set of lies that keeps you thinking you are inferior or descended in some way.

Why are you told these lies?

There is a good reason for it and I explain it in this book in more detail. The important thing here is, if you are having difficulty with the things that I am saying but still want to move forward, control your thinking. Recognize that you have adopted patterns of seeing the world and that it is these patterns that are now being *invoked* by the words on this page. It is these patterns that are blurring your vision or interfering with your concentration.

If you are having difficulty, here is a way to ease your mind.

Know this.

There are no wrong choices here.

You can keep these patterns of thinking if you want. Nothing bad will happen to you now or in some future hell if you do. You will just live your life the way your living it now. You'll eventually transit this physical body (like everyone does) and maybe take another body here or somewhere else.

That's it.

That is all there is to it.

That will be the end of it.

You won't be "judged" for choosing incorrectly.

There's no wrong choice here.

You are free to live however you want and God will love you no matter what you do.

But I will say this.

There is a better way on the other side of the grand illusions of this 3D world. There is a better way on the other side of the cosmic battles between good and evil and the vicious struggles for survival that you fight. There is a promised land of milk and honey and it is just around the corner waiting for you. The nice thing is, you do not even have to get out of your chair to get there. You do not need to change jobs or change families or leave anybody behind. The promised land is inside you and all you have to do to get it out into the world around you (i.e., manifest it), is control those patterns long enough to let me show you the way to remember.

It is not that hard and the payoff for remembering who you really are, among many other things, is high self-esteem and better control over your life.

It is just around the corner.

If you are ready, step forward.

Step onto the spiritual path and remember.

Now if you are still here, congratulations. If you were trained in standard church and scientific ways of thinking, the first obstacle (which is opening your heart and mind to the possibility that there is a better way) is the first and most difficult step. Beyond this it is just a matter of working through things. We have got lots of time to do it and so we'll take our time. As noted, we will start in this book by revealing the basic spiritual truths of this planet. As we progress through this book we will learn to see that many of our beliefs and values, and many of the accepted wisdoms and truths that we have held so dear are at best a benign illusion and at worst the outcome of concerted attempts to keep us in ignorance and darkness. It is going to be an interesting personal process.

Depending on your spiritual and scientific background, my work may mean a total revision in the way you think about things but if you keep an open mind, it shouldn't that difficult to get your head around it because, in fact, I'm not teaching you anything you don't already know.

In fact, if you got that third eye chakra open and running even a little bit, you will probably get the strange feeling that you knew all of this material all along, anyway.

And indeed you did!

This book was not written to introduce you to new knowledge. It is really a sort of summons written to remind you of what you already know. This book is your call to remember your purpose here. It is your invitation to reclaim your birthright and take back your full creative power.

It is time!

Remember who you are.

Remember your purpose.

Rejoice and accept this invitation to a grand spiritual party.

No matter what you think you have done, you are welcome at this party.

Trust me, you are ready.

There is no danger to be found in moving forward.

Remembering who you are, and taking your personal power back puts you in control so step forward now.

The time for living in darkness is over.

The time for living without power is done.

The time for kneeling before priests and bowing before authority is over.

It is time to reclaim your true glory as co-creator and Spark of the Original Creator consciousness.

This is you standing at the door.

Congratulations on finding your way this far.

Welcome Home!

CHAPTER ONE:
THE ENERGY OF THE ASCENSION

When one knows that
The Great Void is full of chi,
One realizes that
There is no such thing as nothingness.

Chang Tsai

The Ascension

Chances are you are here reading these words either because you have accidentally come across this book, you have heard people talking about The Ascension and want to learn more, or you are a seasoned new-ager looking for a clearer explanation of the process of ascension. If you are here for any of these reasons, or just here to learn more about what the new age really means, you have come to the right place.

The Ascension is a popular subject these days and for a very good reason. We are now, at this instant, going through the process of ascension. By "we" I mean all life forms on this planet (human and non-human). Even the earth herself is now ascending. Those who have been anticipating this event are quite excited about it and what it will mean for the whole of creation. There is good reason to be excited. The events that are unfolding now are of universal proportions.

If you are just entering the new age spectrum, you might have the idea that The Ascension is a new topic of discussion. This is not true. The Ascension has been a topic of conversation on this earth for as long as there have been humans to discuss it. Even though they do not use the word "ascension," all major religious systems have something to say about it. Even, perhaps especially, esoteric doctrines (those doctrines where they intentionally obscure the truth to prevent premature access to the knowledge) discuss it. In fact, there is little doubt that at some point in your life you will not have come across some discussion of The Ascension in some form.

Although all have been exposed to the topic of ascension in some form, many of the more spiritually minded among you will have given The Ascension more thought. Those of you who have thought about it will probably understand The Ascension in individual terms. This is no fault of your own. Most doctrines that refer to the process, and most people who care to write or teach about it, speak about The Ascension as if it is an individual process. You are supposed to attain enlightenment. You are supposed to be resurrected from the death of consciousness. You are supposed to attain nirvana.

You you you.

All this talk of "your ascension" is partially correct. The Ascension is about an individual ascension and the return of a grander consciousness (we call it Christ consciousness) into the body. However, The Ascension is much more than just an individual ascension. At its core, The Ascension is really about the entire physical universe. This element of The Ascension, that it is a universal process, is usually left out of all except the most esoteric doctrines. This bears repeating. The Ascension is really a universal event. It is about us, all life on this planet, the planet itself, the solar system, and all things in this universe. In its full magnificence, the event transcends even the boundaries of this universe. However, that is not our concern in this book.

At this point, you are probably wondering just what sort of event on earth (or in heaven) can claim such a glorious and universal status. In order to understand why The Ascension is such a grand event, and to understand its implications for you, you have to first understand a little bit about the way the universe is organized and how we (as Immortal Spirit) create within it. As a start, we will need to uncover for you the nature of the universe. This seemingly difficult task, this grand cosmic enlightenment you are about to experience, is not so difficult and grand at all when you learn that the universe (and indeed all of creation) is really about energy and The Ascension is itself simply an energetic event.

The Universe is about Energy

What is it about energy that is so important to The Ascension process? The first thing you will need to consider is that the universe consists only of energy. Energy is the sub-stratum of all physical manifestation. You could say "light" and you would still be correct because, as we know, light is just energy. However, the term energy is more descriptive and it carries more of the implication that we control the energy just like we control the amount of power we use in our lives. Energy is all around us and it dances to our command. In fact, we have total control over the energy in our lives. We can make it do whatever we want. We can form it, shape it, alter it, move it around, etc.

We use energy to create in some obvious ways as when we use electricity to power a saw that cuts the wood that builds a table. We also use energy in less obvious and more spiritual ways as well.

Spiritually, the process of creation with energy is simple. To create, we think about something and give our intent to create that thing. As we give our intent, we draw from the universal pool of creative energy. As we think (and rethink), the energy begins to move and transform and eventually, whatever it was we were thinking about, whatever is in our consciousness, becomes a physical reality. The whole process involves the gradual slowing and condensation of energy into matter. This is not really news. Physicists themselves understand that matter is

21

simply solidified energy. The only new thing here (and it is not even that new because scientists are beginning to clue into this fact)[3] is that we control the way energy manifests through our intent.

It is as simple as think about it, and it is so.

Of course, right now you are looking around you and asking yourself why you cannot manifest your desires in exactly the way I have suggested. You are thinking if what I am saying is correct, you should be able to materialize a nice cup of coffee and a cinnamon Danish right this instant.

There is a good reason for why things do not manifest instantly in this dimension and that is simply because that while in this body, we are working at a low level of creation. Indeed, we are working at the lowest level (or dimension) there is. As scientists are beginning to realize, the process of creation (energy transmutation) does not just occur on a single dimensional level. Creation occurs in multiple dimensions simultaneously. This means there is a lot more going on around you than you realize. In fact, there are entire life streams that exist all around you that are invisible to you. Although they do try to communicate with us (crop circles for example) we have not reached the vibrational level where we are able to perceive them with the senses of our body. That day is coming though and when it does come that will be the day we meet our rich mythological heritage face to face.

The idea of multiple dimensions that exist simultaneously in the same physical space is important for our discussion for although energy always responds to our creative intent, it does not do so in the same fashion in every dimension. At the highest levels (or dimensions) of creation, the energy we use is very responsive. The energy is energetic, of high "vibration," and close to the Source. As a result, the physical

---

[3] See for example the **Global Consciousness Project** (GCP) at Princeton University http://noosphere.princeton.edu/

world remains very responsive to our creative whims. If we think about a glass of water, there it is. If we imagine a crystal palace, voila. The trade off is simple. Although in the highest dimension the physical world is created instantly from intent, it is also extremely insubstantial. If you stop thinking about what it is you are manifesting, it simply dissolves away.

As we progress down the Tree of Life, the parameters of creation change. As we move energy and physical creation away from the Source, its vibration slows and it becomes less energetic. As this happens, it becomes less responsive to our intent. It also becomes thicker and denser (more viscous, harder, etc.). The responsiveness and density of physicality in any particular dimension is a function of its spiritual rate of vibration. Its vibrational rate is in turn a function of the dimensional distance from the Source. The farther we are from the Source, the less responsive. We might say $R=1/Ds$ where R is the responsiveness of matter and Ds is distance from the Source. Conversely, density is directly related to distance from the Source. We might say $D=Ds$

There it is. There are several dimensional levels of creation and we, as Immortal Spirit, create physicality in all of them down through several vibratory levels until – presto! – the material world you see around you pops into existence. Conceptually it is a simple process and we can see analogues of the process all around us. Consider the change of state from gas to liquid to solid as one example of how matter solidifies as the vibratory rate of energy is slowed.[4]

---

[4] It is probably important to note that the process of creation is a literal process. You get what you think about. This is so even if you think in negative terms. If you think for example that you are stupid, you will draw situations to yourself that help you to experience this thought. If you think you are unworthy, you will draw energy that helps you to experience that as well. Just think of Aladdin and the little bundle of power in the bottle that responds to wishes in an annoyingly literal fashion.

This is the process of creation. You slow down the energy of creation until you get physical matter and you do it through multiple dimensions until you get to a point where it is slow, dense, hard, and unresponsive to intent. The physical world you see around you is the lowest vibration we can attain without all movement coming to a complete standstill. In other words, we cannot go farther because if we did, creation (movement) would cease. Obviously, we do not want that.

There is a visual representation of this creation process in the Jewish Cabbala known as the Tree of Life. You can see the process of creation at several levels (the middle trunk of the tree) as it moves from the top (Kether) through Tiphareth and Yesod all the way down to this earth (Malkuth).

This Tree of Life is a great visualization of the multidimensional process of creation and its staged nature. It should be noted however that the crown is not the Godhead as many suggest. It is simply the first level of creation. Spirit (God) exists as the whole thing and is not separate from it at any level.

You can think of each stop on the way down as a different quantum level of creation. Each level operates in a stable state and each has energetic boundaries that must be penetrated before the process can continue. Moving between these levels means building up energy reserves or momentum in order to pop through the barriers. This process has been going on for eons. However, we are getting ahead of

---

As a species, we are beginning to awaken to the idea that how and what we think is important. If you have been following the self-help literature, it is apparent that people writing the self-help books have recognized the power of intent and the impact of intent on physical and psychological (body and mind) healing. It is now widely recognized that *affirmation* (things like "I am a good person" or "I am worthy") repeated often are extremely powerful catalysts for personal change. If you want to change your life, simply express your intent. Give it a voice since this all works much better if you speak your intent.

ourselves here. Before we go into the details of creation, let us first discuss in more detail the last level of the Tree of Life represented by Malkuth – the physical world you live in now.

Figure One: The Tree of Life

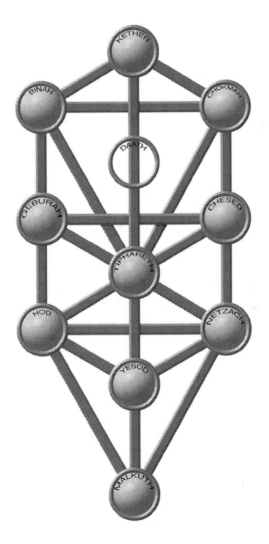

The Physical World

As you might gather, the world down here is an interesting thing. We all have our ideas about it. Sadly, some of these ideas are quite twisted. Many people (for example some priests and scientists) will tell you that this world is worthless, evil, meaningless, and spiritless and we have come simply to dominate it. This myth is prevalent in certain religious systems (God gave "man" dominion over the earth) and in certain interpretations of the scientific theories of Darwin. Although I do not want to get into an argument over evolution (of course we evolved) or the age of the universe (of course it has been here a long time), you should know that Darwinism has been twisted so as to provide a secular alternative to the now discredited creation myths in the bible that defame this level of creation.

None of the mythical structures that defame this world hold any truth. Neither is the human body more than the animal kingdom nor is the earth and this world inferior or profane (needing our control, for example). Nor (it should be obvious) are we and this earth simply the random product of evolution. Given both the planet and our bodies are only crystallized energy like everything else, it hardly makes sense to think of one or the other as "better" crystallized energy. Nor does it make sense to think the earth or these lower dimensions are somehow more profane than higher dimensions. Just because we are down here in the low vibrations does not mean the world is any less important, less exalted or less worthy of our respect than the higher realms we moved in from. It is not. All this talk of hierarchy and control simply reflects and justifies worldly ideas about these things and not the truth of Immortal Spirit.

The truth is simple. All you see around you is simply the creation of Immortal Spirit.

It is ours and we are responsible for it.

However, even though the physical world is "just" what we created, we should not undervalue it or our bodies (as some ascetics like to do) because it is not really "just" the physical universe. The physical world in this dimension is really the crown jewel of creation and we are its creators and protectors.

Indeed, this physical universe is unique in all of creation. It is, as we now know, the most "physical" of all our creative dimensions. In other words, it is the most substantial, hardest, most "real" universe that we have among all the dimensional levels. Partly because of its density, and partly because it is the outcome of many eons of spiritual creative practice, it is the most stunningly beautiful thing we have ever created. The stars, the galaxies, the planets, the flowers, the animals, the birds, the breezes, the tastes, the smells, and even the slugs and the snails, everything here is unlike anything at any of the higher vibrational levels. Nothing we have ever created surpasses this as a playground for Spirit.

Nothing!

This is an amazing treasure. If you pause and consider this, you will see how terrible the myths of its inferiority really are. You will also understand how deep the **crime** of its destruction really is.

The only "problem" with creation down here in the lower vibrational levels is the one I have already noted. Creation here is limited. It is not limited in the sense that its potential is limited. That is not so. We can still create whatever we want down here. The limitations are of a different nature. Creation at this level is limited by its density (or what we may more accurately call inertia). It is very hard and cold down here. Moving the energy around and creating things in this thick soup is much like getting a long train started on its track. It takes intense concentration and effort to get the train going in the direction you want. Once it is going, it moves with relative ease so long as you stay on track. However, if you want to change the direction, or move onto a different track, you have to slow the train down, move it over, and start it up again. The lower you are in the dimensional matrix, the heavier your train and the more effort this requires.

Creation down here is also limited by its sensitivity. The subatomic particles that make up this universe are very fragile. They pop into and out of existence very easily and they must be constantly bound by Spirit or they would just disappear. At the same time, because Spirit is so powerful, we cannot bring to bear the full force of our creative intent because matter would just explode if we did. Therefore, we have to be patient. We get our train started slowly and we move it along and change its direction carefully. We do this without bringing to bear the full conscious light of Spirit into physicality.

At least, that is the way it has been in the past.

An interesting event is occurring now. You see if you can lower the vibrational frequency of energy through stages until you get physical matter, it is also possible to raise the vibrational frequency if you can meet certain conditions. This means that once we have created the hard cold physical universe down here, we can begin the process of raising it back up to a higher dimensional vibration. Take a quick glance at the Tree of Life again (Figure One). The process is represented by taking Malkuth and moving it back up to the level of Yesod (and later from Yesod to Tiphareth). It is a difficult process but it can be done.

This is an interesting phenomenon. The more we succeed in raising the vibrational state of matter up through the dimensions, the more easily it responds to our creative intent. This, of course, is not the same as using a hacksaw to cut a pipe. It is actually about changing the physical arrangement of atoms to reflect our deepest creative intent in a way that is more like the sort of thing we were used to at the higher levels. This means that as this universe ascends into the next vibrational level (and the next after that), we will manifest our thoughts faster and with much more ease and grace. The beautiful thing about this is that as we raise the vibration of physicality, we do not lose the key benefits of creation at this low level. That is, we get to keep its permanence, density, and beauty.

Raising physicality is the goal anyway. Most religions will have something to say about this and they will say it with more or less clarity. They will call it the creation of heaven on earth, or the return of matter to Spirit, or the emergence of Shambhala or something like that. It is also expressed as the return to Godhead. It does not really matter what it is called; the idea is the same. Raise matter up through the dimensional levels so that our creative intent can be easily manifested. This way, we bring the physical world back to the Spirit world.

Exciting is it not?

It should be immediately obvious why we would want to do this.

It will be fun, but also scary for some, and dangerous for others.

It will of course not be dangerous to your soul. That is immortal and indestructible. It will however be quite dangerous for the body. If your dominant method of interacting with the world is negative, that is, if you exist in hatred, anger, jealousy, or any of the other negative emotions, or if you exist out of balance, then as you follow along with the ascended universe, you will manifest this negativity and imbalance both in your immediate environment and in your body very quickly. This means that any illnesses you get will progress faster and with more vigor. It will also mean that unless you clean up your thinking, your life could be an unending roll of personally manifested chaos, confusion, disease, and finally death.

It will be scary because of some of the entrenched beliefs that have been put in place to prevent you from accessing the full power of your body. As you will learn in later chapters, there has been a concerted effort to keep you in fear and illusion. Once you begin to wake up to the truth of your incarnation here and move forward, you will have to overcome the fear placed in you by a system designed to keep you in emotional, psychological and spiritual bondage. You will have to overcome your own sense of unworthiness and claim your status as co-creator of this physical universe.

This will not be easy for many of you. The fears you have to walk through are very deep. Ironically, the self-esteem that will help you walk through your fear has been under attack since your first day on this earth. You have been told, either directly or subtly, that you are worthless, dirty, stupid, and immature. You have been told you are children needing constant tutelage and guidance and, interestingly, that this guidance comes from the authority figures in your life (priests, bosses, or parents). You have also been warned about the judgment of authority. You have been told you will fail if you do not do your job, fail if you do not study, and be subjected to eternal damnation if you do not listen to God. All this nonsense you have been filled with has built up layers of fear that make you afraid to look at yourself.

Unfortunately, until you can look at yourself, you cannot see yourself for who you really are – a being of incredible light and beauty. Sadly, you have been taught to be afraid of your own light and whenever you are confronted with it, you flee from it in abject terror. This state of affairs would be a terrible affront to God if there were not a divinely sanctioned reason for placing you in spiritual bondage. We will discuss this divinely sanctioned reason for your own spiritual castration later. For now you need to be aware that as The Ascension progresses, all of us must overcome our embedded fears and misconceptions. We no longer have a choice in this matter. You can go a long way towards overcoming your fears by thinking about and writing down what LOVE really means and remembering that God is Love and God does not judge, damn, command, or create subservient beings for the purposes of some mad torture game.

Anyway, to return to our discussion, as stated, our goal in this physical universe is to raise the vibration of matter and return it to a higher dimensional vibration.

We call this The Ascension.

Now, while The Ascension is conceptually uncomplicated, in practice it is quite delicate.

For example, it takes a lot of energy to create even at the higher dimensional levels where creation is ephemeral and fluid. As you descend the Tree of Life into the lower dimensions, the energetic requirements expand exponentially. Down here, even doing the simplest things like creating the lighter physical elements (hydrogen, helium, etc.) takes loads of energy and tons of effort. The energy and effort required to create is even greater as you move up the periodic table of the elements. Heavier elements (like uranium) require much more concerted spiritual intent to create and much more energy to keep them together than a simple hydrogen atom. In fact, there is not enough energy available to keep elements that are heavier and more complicated together. Uranium and higher elements are unstable and decay to stable forms as they release the energy that was being used to hold them together. This energy thing and the difficulty of holding creation together works on the evolutionary ladder as well. Simpler life forms require less energy and less intent. However, by the time we get to complex biological life (of any form) the energy requirements are truly staggering.

As I have already noted, the energy requirements of creation are also greater around ascension boundary points. These boundary points are like quantum stages through which creation must pass on its way down (descension) and up (ascension). These boundaries provide points of resistance for creation. It is like breaking the surface tension on a glass of water. It takes just a little extra effort to pierce the barrier but once you are through, the sailing is easy at least until you get to the next barrier. You also get a little extra energy after the barrier is pierced (built up kinetic energy you might say).

It should now be apparent as to what we have incarnated on this earth to accomplish. The basic spiritual problem for us is how do we generate enough energy to raise physicality up to the point of ascension and pierce the quantum boundary that keeps this physical universe from vibrating at the next highest vibrational (dimensional) level. To put it in slightly different terms, how do we draw enough energy from the universal pool to carry the body of Christ (that is the entire world here - the whole world - slugs and all) into ascension so that we will not have to work so darn hard to enjoy ourselves.

Of course, being Immortal Spirit and Sparks of The One we already know the answer to this. The difficulty has been in the implementation details. However, in order to understand the mechanics of this and the difficulties we have faced, we will need to take a closer look at the composition of the universal pool of creative energy.

The Yin and the Yang of It

The question before us is this. How do we draw the energy we need to push physical creation past the quantum boundary point and into ascension? The answer is quite simple. We do this by turning up the polarity of the creation energy. I have already said it takes energy to create. This

much is true. However, it is only partially true. We have yet to speak about the character of the energy of creation or the way it is used to create the universe. A more complete discussion of energy would have to point out that energy exists as an integrated duality. Asian cultures have this aspect of energy perfectly expressed in the yin/yang symbol.

Consider the yin/yang image for a moment. The entire circle represents the energy of creation. It is the entire available pool of energy. As it exists untapped, the energy is neutral or in balance. However, we do not use the energy of creation in its neutral form. We split it into a positive and negative aspect. As this energy manifests, we get the polarities of creation. We get male and female, father and mother, proton and electron, sun and planet, black and white, night and day, and any of a virtually infinite number of opposites. We get, in short, duality.

This duality is very important because it is only in the separation and synthesis of opposites that creation manifests. Although this is a simplification, we can say that we use the positive component as the spark or energetic drive that "goes forth and expands." We use the negative component as the formative mold that catches the spark and shapes it into something interesting. Bringing these two energies together is how creation manifests. Again, these ideas are expressed in symbolic form in the yin/yang symbol.

You will recall from our earlier discussion of dimensions that creation at the different vibratory levels has different characteristics. Lower levels require more effort. Higher dimensions less. Manifestation at lower levels sticks. Manifestation at higher levels is ephemeral. We can now understandably state that in the higher dimensions, our intent can be manifested with a more balanced use of energy. At the highest levels, energy is close to source, vibrates quickly, and is responsive to thought. We need a small amount of the positive yang to get the ball

33

rolling and the same amount of the negative yin to form and shape. However, the necessary polarity is minor. The energy we use is *in balance* with the yin and yang occupying about the same energetic space.

As you know, the conditions for creating physicality change as you descend the levels of creation. As vibration slows and creation forms ever increasingly solid forms, creation requires more energy in general and more yang within that increased flow. It makes sense intuitively. If you need to push a boat through water, you do not require a lot of force. However, put the same boat on land and you immediately require more energy to move it. It is the same with our creation. The lower we move in the vibratory dimensions, the more it is like pushing a boat on land. The lower we get the more force we need. In order to get the extra force we need to push our boat in increasingly difficult circumstances, we must adjust the balance of energy. We generate the extra force we need by using more yang.

How we balance the energy in manifestation will depend on the particular requirements at each dimension and the stage of our creation. If we need a little extra positive oomph (as we do in the lower dimensions), we will turn up the masculine side. If we need more feminine (as for example when we rebalance energy after working with extra yang), we turn up the feminine. If we only need a balanced polarity, we do that.

Simple, right?

One other noteworthy point is that although you can change the balance of energy, you cannot change the total amount that is available. The total energy you draw is a constant. That is, for any given quantity of energy, you can have a certain amount of yang and a certain amount of yin. However, no more than the total (T) you started out with is ever available. This has some important implications not the least of which is that if you turn up the balance on the positive side you *weaken* the negative side. You still have the same amount (T) of energy though. This is perfectly represented in the yin/yang symbol. As the yang side (the creative get up and go masculine side) gets stronger, the yin side gets smaller. However, the total energy remains the same.

Although this might seem odd at first, you can understand this better by visualizing the total (T) energy you are working with at any time as contained in a large bucket. The color of the water in the bucket (either white, black, or some shade of gray) indicates the relative energy balance. If you want to turn up the yang, you add white paint to the water and the water's color (or balance) changes. If you want to rebalance the yin, you add black paint. In neither case does the volume of water in the bucket change. However its color does.

As an important aside, if you consider the metaphor of the bucket and the yin/yang symbol you can see that thinking of the energies as separate or in a hierarchical fashion (male is superior to female) is senseless. The energy itself is just energy and no matter how you balance it, the energies are part of the same root. Black or white, male or female, mother or father, they are the same energy. Racists and sexists take note please. It is the same energy!

Understand?

It should be apparent where this is going. Remember our basic spiritual problem at this dimensional level is generating enough oomph to break through The Ascension boundary and raise physicality back up the Tree of Life. Now you can understand how we do that. We turn up the balance of yang. When we do that, the sparks quite literally fly off our spiritual fingertips from the extra force that is generated by the out of balance yang.

Unfortunately, there are problems. The energy of creation is not something to be trifled with and even a moderately out of balance use of energy can have startling and difficult consequences. As a result, we have to be careful as we adjust the energetic balance. We will take up the wider implications of energetic rebalancing in chapter three.

Conclusion

You now have a basic understanding of the meaning of life as well as a good conceptual overview of the physical mechanics of the process of ascension. As you have learned, creation is simply an energetic process that involves passing through quantum energy levels from high vibratory states to low vibratory states and vice versa. The benefit of going down through the vibratory levels (descension) is that we get increasingly physical manifestations of our intent. The cost is that creation requires more energy and the reality we manifest no longer responds as quickly or effortlessly to our intent.

Fortunately, we are not forever limited by the inertia and unresponsiveness of physicality at this low dimensional level. We can, with the proper effort, take our physical creation and move it back up the dimensional ladder. This involves passing more energy into our creation in order to raise its vibrational rate and push it through the quantum boundary that separates dimensional levels. This is The Ascension. The benefit of this ascension is that while physicality retains its hard physical character, it will not require as much effort to manifest. As ascension proceeds, we gain the benefits of creation at higher dimensions and the benefits of creation at lower levels.

We get the best of both words.

We have our cake and eat it too.

Technically, this process of ascension has already occurred. You have already succeeded in exciting physicality and pushing it through the lowest quantum boundary. You can see evidence of this all around you in the accelerated manner in which your intent is manifested. The easiest way to see this is to consider the physical dimension of time.

Everyone knows that time has appeared to have sped up. More things happen, more discoveries are made, and more things are created in much less time than before. Time is compressed people say. This compression is quite real and is symptomatic of the fact that our physical universe now moves faster than it did before. Time will continue to compress for a bit longer. However, as we all catch up with the ascending earth and realize that living now takes less effort, our perceptions of time will normalize.

The real challenge for us now is not ascension but awakening. As ascension proceeds, the reasons for your ignorance and fear no longer hold. We will examine the reasons for your fear and imposed ignorance when we discuss the problems associated with previous ascension attempts. However, at this point it is worthwhile for you to start clearing away the fear and illusion that have kept you from remembering who you really are if only because if you do not, under the new conditions of the ascended universe, your illusions and fear will manifest in physicality quickly and with considerable force. If you want to participate in glory and ascend without fear and negative consequences, move forward. To do this, simply express your intent to progress. Recite this simple affirmation several times a day.

"I wish to move forward. I choose life. I choose The Ascension."

Then hang on for the wild and glorious ride that awaits you.

CHAPTER TWO:
TIME, THE UNIVERSE, AND EVERYTHING

Dance, then, wherever you may be,
I am the Lord of the Dance, said he,
And I'll lead you all, wherever you may be,
And I'll lead you all in the Dance, said he.

Sydney Carter, Lord of the Dance

Introduction

In the last chapter, we introduced the concept of The Ascension and explained it in energetic terms. We noted that The Ascension is a quantum event that involves moving physicality up through the energetic boundaries that separate dimensional levels. As we discovered, The Ascension is a desirable event because as it proceeds, our ability to manifest intent will be enhanced.

Unfortunately, attaining ascension is difficult. Getting this planet and this universe to the point where we can ensure a safe transition has involved much trial and error. We will discuss our failed attempts and this current successful attempt in subsequent chapters. However, before we proceed to that discussion, it will be helpful to take a detour and discuss in some detail the nature of this physical universe and in particular the nature of time. There are two reasons for this detour. One is that our common conceptions of time, while not completely erroneous, are colored by the limited perspectives we have while in body. While in body and awake, we are very much like a fish inside a cast iron fish bowl. We cannot see outside the bowl and even when we do, it is very difficult to express in words what we have understood. The second and related reason is that any advanced understanding of spiritual topics, like ascension or past lives for example, requires a better understanding of time.

The reason you cannot develop a deeper understanding of things spiritual without understanding time is simple. Without a better understanding of time, we cannot understand the physical universe. The reason for this is because time, like space, is a physical property of this universe and almost all spiritual phenomenon that are relevant to us here on this earth, like ascension, incarnation, rebirth, etc., operate *within* this physical universe and are subject to the laws of physicality. If you do not understand the physical universe, your understanding of things spiritual will be filled with illogic and superstition.

Understanding space is easy. We all understand physical space as the distance between two points plotted on a three dimensional grid. We know there is space between you and this page and between the page and the floor. If we drew a three dimensional grid in the space around you, we could plot the three points (you, paper, floor) in relation to each other. We understand space and are comfortable in it because we have been "in it" since we entered into incarnation on this earth. In the case of space, our lived experience does not interfere with higher spiritual understandings.

The same cannot be said of our understanding of time. It is more difficult to understand and more prone to confusion. The problems arise not so much because we are limited in our ability to understand or that the concept of time is inherently difficult. Time is actually quite easy to understand once you have managed the proper perspective. Unfortunately, getting the right perspective can initially be quite difficult because our lived experience of time locks us in a box and prevents us from seeing outside of the limited perspective of the box.

I realize that in this chapter I am probably going to step on many intellectual and theoretical toes. However, despite the risks I am going to try to provide a perspective on time that un-boxes your brain and helps fit together disparate physical and spiritual phenomenon. I hope that by the end of this discussion you will have the tools necessary to develop a deeper understanding of spiritual phenomenon in general and ascension in particular.

Life, the Universe, and Everything

Let us start our discussion by considering the mundane perception of time we all share. Let us call the mundane perception of time we get while in body *Physical Time*. When we are operating in our physical body, physical time *impresses* us in a certain way. For example, while we are in body, we feel and see that time operates in an inexorable, forward moving, and linear direction. The past is stretched out behind us back to the edge of the universe when the big bang first vibrated this dimension of physicality into existence. Our bodies exist in the present or at the forward edge of time and beyond the forward edge there is the future which we see does not yet exist. For us the future is an unspecified potentiality that unfolds as a result of our past and present actions.[5]

As I have already said, our experience of physical time is limited. Let us call our unlimited experience of time Spiritual Time. Unlike our bodily perspective, Spiritual time is normally known and understood

---

[5] We have of course known (and felt) since Einstein that time is relative. This is true. Time is relative. It is relative to your position in this universe and to your position in relation to higher realities. Although we might want to think that the relativity of time leads one towards higher spiritual understandings, it does not. The relativity of time fits well within the physical properties of this universe and is hence part of our mundane understanding of this universe.

only when you are without your body. That is, you can only understand spiritual time by either being in a position outside of the physical universe or learning to take that perspective while in body. Taking a perspective outside the physical universe is not as weird as it might first sound. In fact, as Immortal Spirit, this is our natural state of existence. At our soul level, we all find our home outside the physical universe and hence outside of time. It is only while in the body that we are inside the physical universe and surrounded by space and time. If you examine the figure below you will see this illustrated visually by the space/time tube.

In this rendering, the left hand column indicates the four dimensional physical universe. Because we are trying to represent four dimensions within a two dimensional line drawing, you will have to imagine that the x-axis (horizontal) represents the three dimensions of space (x,y,z) and the y-axis (vertical) represents the fourth dimension of time (t). Notice in the illustration how the tube stretches back and forth into the three dimensions of space and up and down into the fourth dimension of time. Notice also how all these dimensions are contained within the tube. They do not exist outside of the tube.

Figure Two: The Space/Time Tube

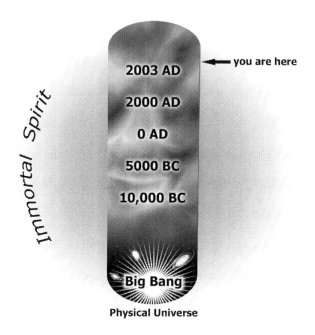

On the other hand we, as Immortal Spirit, do exist "outside"[6] of the physical universe. From outside, the view is quite spectacular. We

---

[6] Although I say that, as Immortal Spirit, we stand outside of physical creation, that is not quite true. Although we have a higher vantage point, we are always in contact with the physical universe. This contact comes about in two ways. On the one hand, we must contain creation within our thought and intent structures. This is quite esoteric but not difficult to capture in words. Spirit must constantly *caress* physical reality with the brush of intent otherwise physical reality immediately begins to disintegrate. This great spiritual truth has been represented, like so many other great spiritual truths, with a simple symbolic design. In the image below, Spirit (the circle) encompasses and contains the physical universe (the square). This is the squared circle. It is a very powerful symbol of awakening and its abuse should not be tolerated.

can see the whole of this universe stretched out in multiple dimensions. We can see the three dimensions of space and the one dimension of time all at the same moment! We can even see the dimensional layers (different vibrational dimensions) stacked up one on top of the other. This makes "adjusting" energetic conditions in the tube quite easy. If you want to know what the energy mix is in 10,000 BC, there it is. If you need to know what is occurring in the higher vibrational frequencies in 100AD, just look. It is all there laid out in front of you in one grand cosmic tapestry.

If our view, as Immortal Spirit, of the physical universe is spectacular, our experience of it is not. In fact, from outside the physical universe, we have no experience of space or time at all. Time, as your brain understands it, simply does not exist outside of the tube. This is evident even in the simple diagram of the space/time tube above. Outside that tube, there are no physical or temporal dimensions. It is probably worth repeating this. Time only exists for us (in the form of a linear, forward moving, duration) while we are in body. Although

---

Spirit Encasing Matter

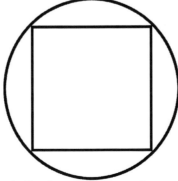

Contact with physicality also comes about when we enter into physicality. This is discussed in the main text.

in body, time seems to have an inevitable, fixed and linear quality, outside and from the perspective of Immortal Spirit, time is nothing more than the distance between two points in the tube.

Our inability to truly experience physicality from the outside leads to one critical limitation of disincarnated Spirit. Although we see all things in physicality, we do not see them like you (a Spirit in body) see them. Physical eyes are a part of this physical universe and if we do not incarnate within the physical universe, we cannot see what you see. We see only colored energy patterns. Where you see anger and hatred, we see browns, blacks, and dirty reds. Where you see love and caring and compassion, we see white, gold, and indigo. We see the entire multi-layered (multidimensional) physical universe as one big swirling mass of energy. We see a multi-colored, multidimensional, scintillating **mind mush** that responds to our thoughtful intent.

Figure Three: The Physical Universe

Given that we can only interact with physicality in terms of energetic patterns, our interventions are necessarily limited. This is where you come in. You, along with many of your Immortal Brethren, have chosen to work with physical reality *from the inside out*.[7] We say that we enter into the body in order to experience and create.[8]

---

[7] Not all souls chose this route because entering in the body is difficult. Not only that but entering here on this earth is seen as quite dangerous because of the possibility of becoming a **lost soul**. A lost soul is simply an individual consciousness that does not remember who they really are or the true nature of the universe **even** after death. These consciousnesses become trapped in the illusions of this world and refuse to see beyond the limited realities that have been a part of this experience here. It can be very difficult to free these souls from their self-imposed ignorance because they are so fearful and paranoid. We often have to gently *cater* to their illusions so that they do not freak out during the delicate transition of death. With the coming of the new age, souls like this will be sent to a sort of inter-dimensional rehabilitation center where their illusions will be carefully stripped away.

[8] There are actually two ways to enter matter. Up until recently, the dominant way of entering physicality in this part of the universe is to actually enter the body with your own consciousness. The other, and safer, way (because you do not risk becoming lost) is to *piggyback* on somebody willing to *let you in*. We might call these Piggy back consciousnesses (PBCs). PBCs are able to experience, with some important limitations, what the body has to offer.

Disincarnate PBCs come in two general types. Good ones and not so good ones. Good ones can be quite helpful and will speed you along your path of spiritual development as fast as you are willing to go. The not so good ones are just lost or damaged souls who are floating around refusing to go one way or the other. They often seek out the type of energy they experienced in their lifetime. Since they are lost, you can bet that they did not experience many good things so they look for the sorts of negative things they experienced. When they find negativity, they hang onto and feed[back] into you that negative energy in whatever way they can. Some will go so far as to try to steer the consciousness of those they choose into directions that enhance the negative energy. I suppose this might be what the church considers demonic possession. Obviously, this is something that you *allow* to happen by *choosing* to exist within a profoundly negative energy field.

If you are aware that these beings exist, you can easily choose amongst the good and bad. Good ones will *never* invade your personal space without your express permission. To activate the good ones, become aware of your spirit guides. You will have between two and five such guides (sometimes more) ready and willing to help your spiritual development. They are an invaluable resource.

The bad ones often hang close by and feed from your energy or find ways to *trick you* into giving them permission to operate at a closer level. To

Spirit may enter into and experience all aspects of physical creation from the rock to the star. However, it is only in an actual body with a brain that Spirit's consciousness can emerge inside of matter. This makes the physical body, and those who are brave enough to inhabit it, very important. Just how important the physical body is will become clear when we discuss your body's status as a manifestation device a bit later.

If you have a reasonable grasp of this new concept of time, you may now be tempted to start saying that everything happens in the "eternal now." You would be partly correct if you said this. However, the problem with this particular way of expressing spiritual time is that it gives the impression that outside of the physical universe there is no duration. This is not true. In the realm of pure spirit, there is duration. However, the duration Spirit knows and works with is different than the duration that is associated with the distance between two points in the space/time tube. To distinguish spiritual time from physical time we can say that as Spirit, we experience creative moments.

What do we mean by the idea of a creative moment? For us as Immortal Spirit, a moment is simply the time it takes to manifest intent. We have "moments" in physicality that are exactly the same as Spiritual moments though we are not normally aware of them as we are usually absorbed in the illusion of linear time. While in physicality, a moment is distinguished by the cycles that bring our intent into physical existence. A moment begins when we express our intent and ends when that intent is realized to one extent or another.

You can think of this in terms of the normal daily activity of making breakfast. When you wake up and you decide (intend) to make breakfast, you enter into your breakfast moment. You grab the bacon,

---

get rid of the bad ones, simply tell them to get lost. They are required to respect your personal space and your intent.

turn on the stove, scramble the eggs, grate the cheese, pour the milk, and make the coffee. When you are finished the process of making breakfast and finished the process of consumption you have completed your breakfast moment. Notice here that you undertake many other activities on your way to manifesting your breakfast. Each of these other activities also represents a moment for you. When you grate cheese, you are having a cheesy moment. When you scramble the eggs, you are having a scrambled moment. If you pause to go to the washroom, you have a bathroom moment (or movement as the case may be).

If you have never made yourself breakfast before, your initial attempts will be clumsy. After all, there is a lot to do and many activities to co-ordinate. However, with practice you will improve. You will find you go through the motions more efficiently and with better results. You grab the jam before the peanut butter because it is closer, you make the coffee first so you have the stimulation, and you do not start the toast until right near the end. Eventually you will stop needing to concentrate and the manifestation will become automatic. At this point the danger becomes that unforeseen events (like burning toast) will interrupt your moment. You do not want that, of course. You never want to lose yourself in your moments so much that you become a danger to yourself and others.

It is very much like this in the spiritual world. We decided to create the physical universe and we decided to ascend it. Obviously, the moments that go into creating physicality are bigger than the moments involved in breakfast, but the idea is the same. Every new cycle (or moment) we "wake up" and begin organizing our activities so that, at the end, we can all enjoy our ascended universe. We grab and evolve the bodies, we create a certain energy balance, we adjust that balance here and there, we send some souls into manifestation to perform some specific tasks, etc. Like our attempts at making breakfast, we do not achieve a perfect result the first time. In fact, we do not achieve even an acceptable result the first few times. Therefore, we rest, rejuvenate, and try again until finally we get everything just right and The Ascension proceeds in the proper divinely sanctioned moment.

There are some important things to notice here about our creative moments. Notice for example the cyclical nature of your breakfast making (you repeat it every day) and how you improve over time. This is the way of creation. Everything is a cycle and all manifestation is circular and progressive (things are "getting better all the time" as the Beatles once said). This is particularly true in the physical universe where we have conducted multiple ascension attempts. While we have failed in the past (sometimes quite miserably), each attempt we made has gotten us closer to the glorious goal of ascension.

I know all this talk of moments and ascension attempts probably sounds esoteric but it is not that difficult. Just think of the "moment" (and indeed the physical universe because it is one infinite collection of *moments*) as one big snake eating its own tail. You have probably seen the symbol in the figure below before. The snake Ouroboros is a graphical representation of the creative moment and, by implication, the physical universe since the physical universe is a collection of spiritual moments.

Figure Four: Snake Ouroboros - The Cosmic Moment

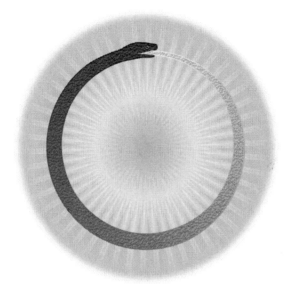

As you can now understand, the moment (large or small) is the sum total of the expressive intent of Spirit. As with our breakfast example, moments exist within moments and pop into and out of existence as our individual and collective intent moves towards manifestation. Picture the space/time tube filled with a thick, multicolored, liquid mind mush. Imagine shaking that tube in your hands. Notice how you get a froth of bubbles large and small? These bubbles are all the moments created by all those consciousnesses actively working with this physical universe (inside and outside). To someone in the middle of things it might look like chaos, but from higher perspectives, you begin to see order coalesce out the perceived chaos. Patterns emerge, bubbles connect and form bigger bubbles, and the whole tube dances a grand cosmic dance of creation. Even in its early chaos it was magnificent beyond words, but as we have gradually learned to work together in creation to help express the highest intent, the tube has literally jumped into vibrant life. It is now alive with intelligent and co-ordinated moments.

To summarize, while in body you experience physical time. You see time stretched out behind you in a straight line all the way back to the start of this universe. This perception of time is valid within physicality but it is meaningless to Spirit. Spirit sees time only as another physical co-ordinate specifying the location of an event. On the other hand, Spirit measures its activities in moments. These spiritual "moments" are cyclic and repeat until intent is manifested successfully. Once a particular creative intent is manifested, new intent and new moments may arise.

I realize your head might be spinning at this point so perhaps you will grab a cup of your favorite beverage and consider what has just been said. Remember, do not get frustrated if you have initial difficulty understanding these concepts. We do not struggle with these concepts because they are difficult or our ability is limited. We struggle because we have never been taught how to leave the limited perspective of bodily consciousness and peer at the universe from a higher level. With practice, your ability to take the unlimited perspective of Spirit will grow.

In the rest of this chapter, I would like to spend some time discussing and demystifying several key spiritual concepts.

Let us begin with your lived experience.

Living in the Moment

For those of you who have ever spent any time researching the new age, esoterica, spiritual, or magical writings, you will know that as you step onto The Path you are invariably advised to live in the moment. Now you will understand why. You proceed much faster and realize your intent with much less effort if you learn to recognize that linear time is an illusion and that cyclical moments are the only real aspect of duration you need to be concerned with. If you want to make a better breakfast, and you want to learn to do it efficiently, pay attention and live in the breakfast moment. Similarly if you want a specific thing manifested in your life, give your intent, hold it, and live in that moment so that you will recognize when things (including new knowledge or lessons) come your way that will help manifest your intent. If you are not aware of your creative intent and not living in your creative moments, do not cry to Immortal Spirit when your toast burns, the walls catch on fire, and your house burns down.

Also remember moments are cyclic. Moments exist and rotate through your life until your intention is realized or you intentionally dissipate intent. You can finesse your creative ability while in body, and indeed understand the things that are happening to you, if you become aware of all the moments you have intended and all the others you are participating in. Learn to be aware of the moments as they cycle in and out of your space in the great creative dance. Some will be your's of course, and some will arise from the intent of others that cross your path because you (or rather your body) are seen as providing an opportunity for assistance. Devote your life to service of Spirit (in whatever you are doing) and your entire life will become a dance of realized creative intent.

Concurrent Lives

By now your understanding of time will have developed to the point where you can easily see that there is no such thing as a past life. How could there be when the past does not really exist? But what, you ask, of all those individuals who have strong and, in many cases, scientifically verifiable impressions of their past lives? Are they dreaming or delusional?

The answer is of course no, they are neither dreaming nor delusional. However, they are also not remembering past lives. What they are getting is brief access to their concurrent lives. As you can probably intuit, concurrent lives are your lives that are being lived in the same eternal moment as the one you exist in now but are simply located at different temporal points in the space/time tube. People who remember or even "see" their past lives have simply managed to pull back The Veil enough to be able to gather information about what is happening with them at other points in the space/time tube.

Figure Five: The Space/Time Tube

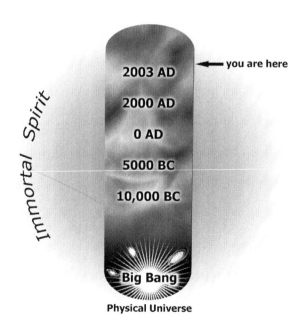

You are probably wondering how you could possibly be in more than one spatial or temporal location at a single moment. In order to understand this you need to understand the structure of your spiritual existence. You are not simply a single point of consciousness. You actually exist in a multi-layered, multidimensional, hierarchical spiritual structure that ascends from your individual consciousness through your higher self, your soul, into the angelic realms, and finally all the way back to God.

You can imagine your entire spiritual self as a tree with trillions of branches all interconnected and all tracing back to the same root structure. At the very tip of each branch are the leaves. These leaves are you. You, as an individual consciousness, are the smallest piece of consciousness (of God) there is. We call you as an individual consciousness the cosmic monad. Of course, you might not feel cosmic or connected to the higher realms at all. The reason is simply that even though the monad represents God split, re-split, and split again, it retains the full power and potential consciousness of God. Until this earth ascends, you cannot enter into this reality in your full power and glory without your body going mad and/or burning up. As a result, you must keep part of yourself hidden away until both you and this world are ready for the higher consciousness. We call the part of you that you keep away from physicality your higher self. If you want a sense of how powerful you really are, try connecting to that. That is your true monad. Your ego consciousness is just a pale and watered down reflection of that.

For the sake of illustration, your ego consciousness might be compared to the tip of the leaf and your higher self the entire leaf. Note as you visualize your monadic leaf how that leaf is connected to a branch along with many other local leaves. All the leaves connected to the same branch form what we might call your soul family. The branch itself represents your soul. Although you are probably used to talking about your soul as if it is a monadic consciousness, it is not. The soul is not a monad. The soul is a spiritual entity that contains hundreds or thousands of individual monads. The soul is a much higher level of consciousness than you are aware of. The soul is the basic guide that sends out its monads into incarnation to accomplish whatever task is has set out to do.

Of course, branches themselves are split and join all the way back to the trunk of the tree and all the way down into the root structure. This tree metaphor is quite illustrative of the way the structures of consciousnesses work. Your higher self (leaf) is connected to your soul (branch) which is connected to the angelic realms (trunk) which traces all the way back to the Source (root structure). Visualize this and you will see that you are connected to everything and everyone and, importantly, you draw sustenance from the Source.

You now have enough information to understand how concurrent lives work and how you are sometimes able to sense what is going on in them. Concurrent lives are just other monadic consciousnesses close to your own location on the tree (part of your own soul). When conditions are right, i.e., when you are not repressing your spiritual connections, you may draw information into your monadic consciousness from related monadic consciousnesses. This happens most often with children (who have not yet had their spiritual connections severed) or with adults who are able to pierce The Veil and glimpse into their higher consciousness.

This is quite interesting. Stop and consider for a moment what you might be doing in several of your other concurrent incarnations. You may be experiencing life as a Cathar Monk, a peasant in a field, a king on a throne, a female in labor, or a high priestess in an ancient temple. All this is happening for you right now in this creative moment.

If you think that is interesting, consider the following. You do have access to the knowledge and wisdom gained from all your other incarnations. The experience you get as a Cathar monk can help you, if you allow, with whatever your current endeavors in life are. The same goes in reverse. Whatever experiences you have now can help with your life as a Cathar monk. The soul gains experience from all its incarnations at once. Use your imagination here and envision what happens if you make a spiritual breakthrough in one life. If you can get your head around that you will know that the choices you make in any single monadic incarnation are far more significant than you might think since each experience provides learning and insight for all the other incarnations of your soul.

The End of Time/The End-times

From our brief discussion of the nature of time you now understand that as Immortal Spirit, we have an expansive view of the entire space/time tube. However, we should not think that the space/time tube is infinite. Spirit is infinite. The physical universe is finite. It has boundaries. The lower most boundary of the universe exists at the point when this dimension of physicality first vibrated into existence with the big bang. This is the physical limit of this universe and telescopes will never be able to see past that limit because, being a product of the physical universe, they cannot see outside its boundaries.

The upper boundary of the universe is literally the edge of possibility or the edge of time. Interestingly, the top is affected by everything below. The sorts of creative things you can do at the end of the tunnel (like ascend for example) are very much dependent on the conditions in the tube all the way back to the beginning. The Mayans understood this. They came as spiritual emissaries to remind us where the end of the tube was and why it was important. They originally told us the end of time (the edge of the tube) was 2012. Beyond 2012 they could not see because it simply did not exist. After 2012, time ended. This was not because the universe ended but because the world that they existed in, i.e., the old world with the old energies, ceased to exist. They could not see past 2012 because at 2012 our creation train literally *jumped the cosmic track* and moved onto an entirely different time line. This great leap of possibility that the Mayans foretold was, in fact, the date of the original Ascension and the grand awakening.

Fortunately, since the Mayans first came to identify The Ascension and awakening point, conditions have changed. The fantastic work of the starseeds has allowed the time of ascension to be moved forward. It has also prevented the worst awakening scenarios and now we are able to proceed with far less violence than on previous cosmic tracks. Now, ascension and awaking occur in 2003 and it is during that year we jump the track and begin what many have called the seventh creation.

Unfortunately, the seventh creation is a topic for another book. My purpose here was to simply give you a sense of what all the talk about the "end-times" was all about. As you can see, passing through the "end-times" does not signal creative doom and gloom. However, things do change starting in 2003. Changes have started gradually and subtly but they will inexorably accelerate over the next few months. Just what the new earth will look like in a couple of years we can only guess based on our assessment of the probabilities (see the section on prophecy below). However, we do know the general direction of creation and we are guaranteed a very high level utopian unfolding. When things finally settle down and those currently fighting their 3D demons wake up, it will be an amazing world filled with love, prosperity, and peace.

Prophets and Prophecy

If you can understand time, end-times, and living in the moment, you can now better understand how prophecy works. Let us start by pointing out that there are two types of prophecy. The first type of prophecy occurs when we are standing at the edge of time. If you are standing at the edge of time, you cannot actually see into the future because there is no future and there is literally nothing going on. However, although you cannot see the future, you can still *estimate* the probability of alternative futures. Although the spiritual science of this is quite complicated and gets you deep into signs, cycles, energy patterns, and the like, the basic principle is easy. You look at the conditions throughout the tube, you examine the energetic mix, and you project forward what the mix will look like at specific locations in the tube when it has finally expanded to that point.

Your projections are of course, based on a type of spiritual math and estimation that is very precise and very advanced. You can see that prophecy at this level really is an exercise in probability assessment. We cannot foresee specific events but we can make educated guesses at what will happen with the quality of energy that is now (and will become) available. We might call this type of prophecy, probabilistic prophecy.

The other type of prophecy we might call visionary prophecy. This sort of prophecy occurs when we stand at any point in the space/time tube behind the edge of time. Some will tell you that prophets are able to access something called Akashic Records for this. These Akashas are presumably a record, kept in some great spiritual hall, of everything that has gone on or will go on in this universe.

Obviously, there is no great hall of records or Akashas. Although there is a *Cave of Creation*, this cave only stores a vibrational summary of your existence on this earth. It is not a universal storehouse of information. In terms of prophecy, it is not that important. It does serve a useful purpose for understanding individual lifetimes but other than that its usefulness is limited.

Rather, when we speak of visionary prophecy we need to look at the space/time tube. In order to be a visionary prophet anywhere in the space time tube, all you need to do to be able to see the future (or the past for that matter) is develop a strong link to the spirit world and request a little help from your (disincarnate) friends. It is that simple. Spirit sees everything that is going on inside the tube and so the issue is simply gaining the perspective of Spirit. As Spirit, we can look into 1012 BC or 2000 AD to check out the goings on. If we, in body, want to know what is happening at some moment in the front of the tube, all we need to do is look with the eyes of Immortal Spirit. That is, all we have to do is connect to that part of our self that can see the tube from the outside. When we do that, we may receive a picture of everything that is going on anywhere and anytime in the space/time tube.

Prophecy has been used several times in the space/time tube for some very important reasons. Nostradamus came during a moment when the conditions in the tube were spiraling into chaos (i.e., we were not achieving our ascension goals) and the end-times was a mix of out of control natural disaster, war, disease and death that were reminiscent of Atlantis and symptomatic of a failed ascension attempt. Nostradamus was a special spiritual emissary who came with a sort of progress report on conditions and an appeal to get things under control. Nostradamus came and he essentially said, "get control of the mind mush **NOW** because you are not going to like what is currently happening at the edge of time."

Thankfully, we listened and managed to straighten out and fly right (although we did need warnings again during the sixties and early seventies). Armed with Nostradamus' foresight, and as one moment passed into the next, we were able to alter the conditions and change the future. In fact, all of us in incarnation were so impressed with the message of Nostradamus that we worked our little buns off, succeeded in creating the conditions for ascension, and even foreshortened the tube and brought the point of ascension closer. The change for us has been quite impressive and now, instead of disaster, we have glory.

So, what did we do to change conditions? That is properly a discussion for later chapters but we can note here that we simply stepped up our interventions. At the same time that Nostradamus came with his dire warnings, a universal call went out for assistance and intervention on this earth. This call was answered by starseeds from all over creation who came to provide critical assistance. These starseed interventions, which we discuss in much more detail in subsequent chapters, helped create the conditions necessary for ascension and awakening on this planet.

Conclusion

In this chapter, we took a bit of a detour from our main task in this book (i.e., to help everyone understand The Ascension). Here we learned something about the nature of time and discovered that our bodily notions of time, i.e., its linear, subjective, forward moving sensibilities, do not exist for us as Immortal Spirit. We also learned to distinguish linear time from the way Spirit understands duration as cyclical moments where intent is given and manifested.

We covered considerable conceptual ground in this chapter. Admittedly, I gave only a brief and limited discussion of time and spiritual moments. However, I did provide enough information to get you thinking about the conceptual box that your body places your mind in. As you now know, your understanding of this physical universe derives from your bodily perception or your bodily senses. The problem with this is that you are not your body and if you identify too strongly with it, your ability to understand this universe from a more spiritually advanced perspective will be limited. It is not an understatement to suggest that as you advance on your spiritual path, losing your bodily identification and opening your mind to the higher understandings of Spirit will become increasingly important.

To convince you of the importance of your own efforts to rethink your place in this world, we also spent some time testing your new conception of time by applying it to several seemingly intractable and illogical spiritual concepts like past lives, prophecy, and understanding the end-times scenarios. You can see how the new and higher conception of time introduced in this chapter clarifies and makes logical many of these difficult spiritual concepts that resist understanding while confined to bodily concepts of this physical universe.

In the rest of this book we return to an explicit discussion of ascension and the way we have brought this planet to its current exalted location in the creative scheme of things. However, as we discuss starseed interventions, timelines, prophecy and even your own ascension and awakening process, always try to stay above this earth and within the perspective of Immortal Spirit. Remember, for example, that all starseed interventions at all locations in the space/time tube are happening concurrently and in this grand ascension moment. Bringing forward your new conception of time and physicality will help you understand the increasingly miraculous nature of the changes that are set to unfold on this earth.

CHAPTER THREE:
PREVIOUS ATTEMPTS

You take the blue pill and the story ends. You wake in
your bed and you believe whatever you want to
believe. You take the red pill and you stay in
Wonderland and I show you how deep the rabbit-hole
goes.

Morpheus, from The Matrix

Introduction

In chapter one of this book, we defined and examined The
Ascension process. There we discovered that ascension was, at root,
about energy. We learned that there is a vast pool of balanced energy
available to us for creation. We learned we use this energy, in various
configurations, to manifest our intent. We discussed, in rather general
terms, how this works and learned that energy responds to thought and
that as we think we create. We also learned that the creation process
works in multiple dimensions. At the highest levels our physical
creations are very energetic and very responsive to our intent. As we
descend the Tree of Life, however, energy slows and the resulting
creations are less responsive. They are also more physical. The process
of ascending and descending the Tree of Life moves in quantum stages
with extra effort required at the quantum boundaries and extra energy
released after the barriers have been penetrated.

In chapter one, we also discussed the nature of the energy of
creation. Our discussion of the duality of this energy led us to consider
the beautiful yin/yang symbol. We learned from our examination of
that elegant symbol how energy exists as a balanced unity within which

a potential polarity exists. We also learned that it is possible to take the energy out of balance. Normally, of course, we would want to work with balanced energy. However, for certain creative tasks it is necessary to work with the energy out of balance. Penetrating the ascension boundary is one task that requires more yang-flavored energy.

In this chapter, we extend our discussion of The Ascension by looking at past attempts to bring this universe up to and through the boundary point. As we will see, this is not the first time we have attempted to traverse the boundary from this lowest dimensional level back up towards the Godhead. In fact, we have undertaken three major attempts on this earth.[9] However, before we go into any detail about our major attempts at traversing The Ascension boundary it is necessary to learn a bit more about how the energy of creation works

---

[9] You do not see much of the evidence of these earlier attempts because the physical plane from a certain location upwards in the space/time tube was reconfigured at the end of each attempt. Because of the reconfiguration, much of the *evidence* was submerged or disappeared in the general alteration of the cosmetics of the planet.

However, there is some evidence available for lost civilizations in the ruins of ancient cities or the shallow waters of the great oceans. There have been individuals searching for these records for many decades (Jacques Cousteau was one of the first to take the possibility of lost civilizations seriously). Unfortunately, the voices of these individuals have been suppressed. When suppression has not worked, the suppressors have laid ridicule at the feet of those who take the evidence seriously. When that fails, careers are often ended.

You will not understand the reason for this until a bit later in this book. For now, those who are interested can look for clues to the lost civilizations in our remembrances of Atlantis and Lemuria. These remembrances you can find in your own hearts and in the visions and imaginings of the more *intuitive* or artistic among you. These individuals have shared their glimpses and half sightings of the past attempts with us. Writers often write of past pages or times when the current *energetic configuration* of this earth was different. Consider the epic novel *The Mists of Avalon* by Marion Zimmer Bradley. Arthur C. Clark's *Childhood's End* or Douglas Adam's trilogy in five parts, *The Hitchhiker's Guide to the Galaxy* both speak to the experimental nature of our incarnations on this earth.

and how we, as Immortal Spirit, are able to manipulate it to best achieve the results we intend.

Energy Revisited – A Question of Balance

I suppose the question that pops into your mind at this point is why we have undertaken multiple attempts at The Ascension. Why did our first or second attempt not succeed? The reason for our failures has to do with the way energy works. As I noted, energy comes as a unified pool of balanced potential. We access that universal pool of energy either in balance or with one side of the energetic potential turned up. Our preference is always to work with energy in balance since this is when creation works best. When we work in balance, there is just enough of the expressive and energetic (yang) spark of creation to get the job done and just enough of the formative (yin) to keep things together.

Unfortunately, we cannot use balanced energy at all levels. As we move down the dimensional ladder energy slows. As this occurs, the physical matter it manifests becomes heavier and carries progressively more inertia. In order to overcome this inertia, we gradually have to turn up the balance of yang energy so that we might generate extra momentum and cellular excitation. This is a gradual process. As we descend the Tree of Life, we take the energy of creation and move it increasingly off balance. In this way, we get more of the energetic drive that we need to manifest physicality in the lower dimensions.

There are tradeoffs of course. Using the energy out of balance has an impact on how our intent manifests. The more out of balance, the more obvious the impact. For example, the more yang we use, the more excited our creation becomes. This excitation is expressed in many ways. In the natural world, it is expressed in rapid evolution and energetic fluctuations in nature. In our bodies the energy expresses itself as the typically masculine traits of ambition, drive, competition, etc.

Another outcome of extra yang is an accelerated rate of manifestation. Even without pushing through The Ascension boundary, we can speed up manifestation by turning up the yang energy. The more yang, the more excited physicality becomes, the faster we move, and the less time it takes to accomplish things. We can actually experience this excitation through our subjective perception of time. For many of us living in the excited physical conditions at the end of this ascension attempt, time has compressed itself and we now accomplish far more in far less time. This time compression is partly the result of the extra yang we have floating around.

The unbalanced yang has one other important implication especially when paired against the heavy inertia that is characteristic of physicality at lower dimensions. More yang means it is harder to control our physical manifestations. We can visualize the impact of the yang energy on our ability to control physicality if we again consider the train metaphor we introduced in chapter one. Consider the physical universe at each dimensional level as one long train on a cosmic track. In the higher dimensional levels where energy vibrates quickly, the Train of Physicality (TOP) is small, light, and responsive to our intent. If we want it to move, it accelerates quickly. If we want it to stop (or if we lose sight of it), it stops quickly. The kinetic energy and inertia our TOP accumulates while moving is relatively small. As a result of our small responsive TOP, we do not need much force to get the train moving or alter its speed. A small engine will do.

We can extend this TOP metaphor a bit further to include the formative yin energy. Here, the yin energy is comparable to the tracks that we, as Immortal Spirit, lay to guide the train. At higher dimensional levels, the formative yin energy is stronger and more balanced against the yang. As a result, it is easy to lay the tracks and the tracks easily support the weight of the train. If we want to change directions, our powerful yin makes it easy to push the tracks around or even lay entirely new lines. In higher dimensions with high vibratory rates and balanced energy, creation is thus easy to control.

As you move down the Tree of Life, conditions change. The farther you move down, the more unresponsive creation becomes and the more out of balance we have to make our energy. When you get down into the lowest dimension, the energy has become quite cumbersome and dense. Because of this density, you need much more yang to get things moving. Extending our train metaphor, you might say we need bigger engines to get the train started or to slow it down. Of course, turning up the yang weakens the yin. So just as our train gets heavier, more cumbersome, and harder to start and stop, so also do our tracks (yin) get smaller, weaker and more difficult to lay.

Right away you can see the implications of this. At lower dimensional levels it is harder to get our TOP moving in the direction we want, harder to stop it once it is moving, and harder to alter its direction. If you lay tracks and you decide you do not like where the train is going, it takes a lot of time to slow down, back the train up, lay the new set of tracks, and restart the process. There is also a very real danger of things getting away from us and spinning out of control. For example, if the TOP is moving fast and we suddenly realize that the direction we sent it in leads straight into a brick wall, we may have difficulty stopping the train before it blows itself up against the unanticipated physical constraint (wall).

Obviously, the danger of our losing control increases as our trains get bigger and more powerful and the tracks get weaker and harder to lay. The lower we are in the dimensional mix, the more careful we must be. And we are careful. We, as Immortal Spirit, do not take creation lightly. As we descended the Tree of Life vibrating each new dimension of physicality into existence, we carefully adjusted the energetic balance. We took educated spiritual guesses as to what balance of yin/yang would get the job done and always erred on the conservative side. After all, it was easier to add more yang to the equation than it was to halt a veering and out of control TOP.

Getting down the Ladder of Creation was no big deal. We turned up the yang energy in small increments until we attained the power we needed to jump the boundaries and bring the dimensional universes into existence with the proverbial big bang. Our problems really started when we reached the bottom and we decided we would try to take this low dimensional level of physicality and move it back up the Tree of Life. Even as we initiated our first attempt to traverse the boundary, we knew we would have to be extremely careful. At this level, we are already working with huge TOPs carrying massive inertia running on very weak tracks. Turning up the yang even a little bit puts us on precarious ground.

Yet we are Immortal Spirit and we are undaunted. For our first attempt we turned the yang up just a little bit and quickly got down to the business of creating the conditions we thought would allow us to traverse The Ascension boundary.

Lemuria

Our first attempt at creating the conditions for ascension in this dimension goes by the name of Lemuria. As noted above, ascending the Tree of Life would require more yang than we needed descending the Tree. However, because of the possibility of losing control, we were quite careful about how much extra yang we added. Let us say that for Lemuria we felt safe turning up the imbalance by an additional thirty-five percent.[10] We did not think the imbalance would be enough to allow creation to burn itself out or run off the tracks, but we did hope that there would be enough momentum generated to move physicality through The Ascension boundary.

Our first choice was a reasonable guess and it did bear creative fruit. We got the extra creative drive we needed to get things moving in response to our intent. We got our primordial soups, our early life forms, the evolution of the higher mind, and eventually, as brain capacity grew and the body matured, consciousness in matter emerged. This was exactly what we wanted.

On this planet, the results of the evolutionary push were quite spectacular. As we approached the end of our Lemurian experiment, everything on this earth was about as close to perfect as it has ever been. The ecosystems were perfectly in tune, the animals lived in harmony with nature, and the beauty and variety of life was simply stunning. It is very difficult for us to imagine the beauty and balance of the earth during Lemurian times because under the extremely unbalanced energetic conditions of our last two attempts we have savaged our earth so completely. We simply have no reference point to consider the difference – except perhaps in the imaginative drawings of fantasy artists.

There is much we could say about Lemuria but one of the defining characteristics of that experiment, and one of the most important features for our purposes here, was the felt interconnectedness of all things. Lemurians felt this connection very strongly. It was a lived experience for them. The Mayan saying "In Lak'ech," which literally means "I am another yourself," beautifully captures the profound lived interconnection of all life during the

---

[10] The accuracy of this number is not important. You just need to get a *qualitative* feel for the level of the imbalance.

Lemurian experiment (as we will see later, the interconnection was itself the result of the still powerful influence of yin energy). The level of spiritual understanding and attainment of the Lemurian civilizations was very high. The Lemurians existed in peace, harmony, and abundance. Lemuria was much like the Garden of Eden is reported to have been. There was no fear, little anger, and no hatred. The civilizations of Lemuria were the glorious crowning jewels of physical creation.

There are many remembrances of this early utopia in our genetic memory. It filters into our religions, myths, and songs whenever you hear of the need to "get back" to some earlier, more pristine and innocent existence. Of course, although we all crave and remember (to one extent or another) this sort of society, in general we have a hard time understanding it, appreciating it, or even accepting it. Our society and our way of thinking is so diametrically opposed to the Lemurian way that we fail to recognize it and even belittle and attempt to destroy any evidence of it because it is a deep threat to our current status quo.

To this day, we see remnants of Lemurian society. For reasons that will become clear shortly, after we ended the Lemurian experiment, Immortal Spirit did not totally erase Lemurian culture. If you are interested in getting a glimpse of what a spiritually advanced people look like, look no further than the indigenous and first nations people scattered across all continents of this earth. Their societies are the physical remnants of ancient Lemurian civilizations. Indigenous populations are all genetically connected to the original Lemurian cultures.[11]

---

[11] To give you some sense of what Lemurian society was like, consider these things. In Lemurian society, children were honored. Children were seen as new messengers of the Divine, and not as the empty vessels our society believes them to be. Lemurians did not *own* their children nor did they attempt to fill the children with so much nonsense that they could not

function as authentic human beings. They did not try to shape the children into miniature images of themselves nor did they seek wage slavery for them. Rather, the Lemurians protected the children, raised them as the children of light that they were, and learned from them as the children learned from their parents. It was a beautiful, equitable, and spiritually elegant relationship.

In our society, we fail to appreciate the true beauty of the child. We box them in rooms, teach them subservience and docility, undermine their spiritual connections, and destroy their sense of self. We wish for them a job or a career or some other form of slavery that serves the needs of others and not their own deep spiritual needs or desires. We twist them and break them and then call them functioning adults. This is a terrible joke since by the time they reach adulthood they are so disconnected as to be mere shadows of their original selves. They (we) then spend all our time scrambling to revive our lost sense of connection within dysfunctional relationships and twisted social forms.

There are other differences between our way and the Lemurian way as well. In the Lemurian society, Elders were honored. They were seen and respected for the wisdom they had accumulated over a long life of service to the earth and Spirit. Lemurians understood the true value of life on this planet and the value of the journey. Rather than fearing the destination (death of the physical body) and scrambling to hide away any evidence of that destination, as we do now, they honored the destination and those who had traveled the long miles. Instead of hiding their elders away in fear, they were kept in their communities, honored and provided with productive and meaningful ways to contribute to their communities. Indeed, it was the elders who bore primary responsibility for raising children for it was felt only the elders could be entrusted with such an honor and responsibility of nurturing a young life. Elders remained productive and valuable members of the society as long as they lived.

In our society, we hide our elders away. We believe them to be senile and/or unproductive and we treat them as burdens despite their life long contributions. We place them in homes, forget they have built the society we live in, and ignore any wisdom they may bring to our lives. We force their care onto the backs of a few females rather than making it a collective responsibility. We do this because we have been taught that only a productive individual working in a productive enterprise is a valuable entity. Older bodies are not as energetic as younger bodies and are not viewed as *exploitable* commodities by those in power. We also do all this out of our own fear of death. Because we do not have an authentic spiritual connection, we cannot see death as anything but a termination of the body (our self). In our unholy terror of what should be a beautiful transitioning event, we hide all evidence of it away.

Lemurian society itself also did not honor and worship slavery (productivity) as we do. Lemuria was a beautiful and balanced world where

The civilizations of Lemuria were wonderful, creative, and balanced civilizations. Unfortunately, there was not enough yang to enable us to break through the ascension boundary. Since The Ascension was the only reason for manifesting on this earth, we had little choice but to end Lemuria in this locale by reconfiguring this reality and rebalancing the energy. However, although the vast majority of Lemurian civilization was destroyed, as noted above, enclaves of Lemurian society were spared and the survivors scattered. The hope was that one day when the energy on this earth could be returned to balance, their wisdom and spiritual knowledge would prove useful in the healing process that many would find necessary.

---

creativity and self-expression were the highest goals. Lemurians were not brainwashed to be the servants of others. They did not spend years in school learning that coffee breaks were only fifteen minutes long and lunches one hour in length. They did not spend their years learning to worship authority. They did not tie themselves to assembly lines or desks in rank servitude. Rather, Lemurians were trained to be Sparks of The One and to express their connection and their purpose with dignity, pride and glory. Lemurians never worked in the sense that we understand work. They occupied their time with the things that made their hearts sing. For some it was music, for others it was service. None burdened others and all were independent, beautiful, expressive beings. Each individual existed as they wanted to exist. Unlike the profound distrust of life we all share (the struggle for survival), Lemurians knew and understood deeply in their hearts that abundance and not scarcity was the birthright of all of God's creation.

There was conflict in Lemurian society. There were many enclaves or tribes and they did not always agree. However, the conflict was always minor and there was always the assumption that the other participant in the conflict was a valuable member of the family of Spirit. Lemurians understand that "I am another yourself." As a result, conflict was never entered with the intent of destroying another person and certainly never with intent of destroying an entire tribe. The destruction of even a single individual would have been unthinkable and as difficult as cutting off your own hand.

Energy Revisited – A Question of Connection

Before we turn to an explication of our second attempt to traverse The Ascension boundary, we again need to revisit and expand our understanding of energy. As you now understand, turning up the balance of yang can be dangerous. We used the metaphor of a train to help visualize the implications of too much yang. The more imbalanced things are, i.e., the more of the energetic spark we use, the bigger that train is. The bigger the train, the faster it goes. The faster it goes, the more kinetic energy it accumulates. The more energy, the harder it is to control.

Unfortunately for us, the problem does not end with the train's momentum. As we discovered, there is a catch 22. The more you turn up the yang side of the creative pool, the weaker you make the formative and moderating side. If you turn the balance too far and give the yang too much strength, the yin becomes so weak as to become invisible and ineffectual. This weakening of yin has some profound implications. The potential for losing control over our TOP because of the "kinetic energy" of the train is one such implication of course. However, the problem goes deeper than this. If the yang side becomes too strong, our ability (as Immortal Spirit) to *connect* with our manifestation is impaired. This inability to connect can have very serious consequences.

You will have to pay attention here because this will be difficult to follow. When I speak of physicality in this context I am not speaking of the whole of physicality but rather one special part of it. That part is the human body. As you may or may not have gathered, the human form (and other forms with highly developed brains and nervous systems) is very important in the overall creative process. Advanced life forms (humans, dolphins, etc.) are essentially physical vehicles for Immortal

Spirit. You can think of them like the cars you drive. You enter them when you are awake and you use them to drive your consciousness around in. With highly advanced bodily systems, Spirit is essentially able to enter into physicality and experience it from the inside out. This is your experience right now. You are a conscious monad experiencing physicality with the multiple senses of the physical body.

You are Immortal Spirit futzing around in your bodily vehicle.

The problem for all of us is that you are not aware of yourself as Immortal Spirit. You are only aware of your bodily consciousness (your mind) and nothing else. You have no connection to your higher self, no connection to the consciousness hierarchy that is Spirit, and absolutely no sense of how the spirit world truly operates. Of course, you might believe in God and Spirit and believe in a higher purpose and all that, but for many these are articles of faith and not things they know. You may believe it, but you do not see it. You are disconnected from the Spiritual realm.

It is important to understand that this is not a normal phenomenon. In other parts of the universe, we retain strong and clear connections to our higher selves and the Spirit world even while we are motoring around in our physical vehicles. So why are we disconnected on this earth? The disconnection we endure is essentially a function of the imbalanced energy. The outpouring of yang energy that we must work with to ascend this universe severs our spiritual connection. Just why this disconnection happens will become clear as we go into more detail about the true nature of your physical body.

The Body as a Manifestation Device

Above we suggested that you consider your physical body a vehicle for your immortal soul. There is much truth in this metaphor. However, it is not the whole truth. Your body is a vehicle for Immortal

Spirit but it is not just a vehicle. Your body is not simply a lump of flesh, bones, and dust that you go to parties in and abuse with drugs, alcohol, and processed foods. It is a finely tuned masterpiece of spiritual engineering. When properly tuned, your body allows Immortal Spirit to create in physicality in ways far more powerful and precise than is possible without the benefit of this marvelous physical system.

You will recall from the last chapter how Immortal Spirit standing outside of physical creation (outside the space/time tube) is limited in its ability to perceive and understand physicality. If you are a Spirit and you are not in body, all you see is a tube of multi-colored energetic mush. You can manipulate the energy in the tube but your understanding of the dynamics inside are limited because you cannot **see** what a Spirit in body sees. To overcome this limitation, Spirit created the physical body so that it could enter into physicality, see what was going on, and affect things from the inside out.

In body, Spirit can do many things with physicality that Spirit outside of body cannot. On a mundane level Spirit can work with physicality by, for example, cutting down trees, creating lumber, and building houses. However, the body allows control that is far more creative than even that. In order to understand just how much creative power the physical body has, you have to understand it as an energy system. The body is really an advanced energy-focusing device that allows Spirit to draw down and push out the energy of creation for precise creative manifestation in physicality. Perhaps instead of calling your body a vehicle for Spirit, it might be better to speak of it as a manifestation device.

Just how does this energy manifestation or focusing device work? Well, your body has several energetic toroids or chakras.[12] Each chakra is a multi-dimensional vortex that penetrates all the way back to the

---

[12] The word chakra is Sanskrit for wheel or disk.

pool of creation energy and all the way forward through each level of your body (your astral, etheric, etc.) till it finally exits and manifests in physicality with your bodily organs. These vortexes are very important. They provide a conduit through which the energy of creation may pass into physicality.

The chakras themselves correlate with several aspects of your physical existence including levels of consciousness, developmental stages of life, the colors of the rainbow (ROY G BIV), the seven tones of the major scale, and bodily functions and organs. The seven chakras are the seven seals which when fully open and connected give Spirit total access and total control over this physical reality. A visual representation of the chakra system is provided in the figure below. Table one provides an overview of various chakra correspondences.

Each chakra is a sort of control center. It shapes the energy of creation and allows that energy to be used for certain creative tasks. For example, the third chakra, which is associated with your solar plexus (sun center), allows your body to manipulate and shape the raw energy of creation. This is your personal power center and it is this center that is blocked when we have given away our power to some sun toting deity, king, or politician. Your second chakra is your creative center. This chakra draws from the available pool of creative energy and focuses it into physicality. As this chakra draws and focuses the creative energy, your third chakra provides the authority and direction for that creative energy. Your heart chakra is your overall spiritual control center. It is through your heart chakra that the intent of Spirit is passed. Your root chakra is your grounding chakra and it does exactly what its name implies. It grounds you and completes the energetic circuit.

Figure Six: Chakra System

Table One: Chakra Correspondences

Chakra Seven: Crown.   Functions: Access to unlimited knowledge of spirit. Connection to higher intelligence, spiritual realms.   Dysfunctions: Limited ego consciousness.   Organ=Brain.
Chakra Six: Third Eye/Brow.   Functions: Psychic power center. Seat of expanded vision. Access to personal and higher truths.   Dysfunctions: Limited vision. Egomania. Dogmatism. Limited understanding.   Organ=Pineal Gland.
Chakra Five: Throat.   Functions: Expression of Truth. Guru.   Dysfunctions: Arrogance. Self-absorption. Disrespectful communication. Repression of voice.   Organ=Thyroid/Voice Box.
Chakra Four: Heart/God Center.   Functions: Manifestation Merkaba. Connection to Spirit. Security. Acceptance. Total self.   Dysfunctions: Domination of others. Judgment. Oppression. Lack of self-esteem.   Organ=Heart.
Chakra Three: Solar Plexus.   Functions: Will. Self worth. Personal Power.   Dysfunctions: Giving power to others. Inability to decide or act. Subservience. Domination.   Organ=Solar Plexus.
Chakra Two: Sacral.   Functions: Creativity. Autonomous expression.   Dysfunctions: Self-destruction. Failed creativity. Smothering. Inability to let go.   Organ=Reproductive tract.
Chakra One: Root.   Functions: Grounding. Connection to Source. Innocence, simplicity, joy, play.   Dysfunctions: Mistrust, fear, lost innocence, antagonistic relation to creation.   Organ=Digestive System.

As you can see, each one of these chakras gives your higher self certain *powers* in this world. These chakras are not to be trifled with. They are more real than the illusory world you currently inhabit. Each chakra is powerful on its own but when lined up in a straight line, fully open, and grounded they give you God like powers over physicality. Even from this brief overview, you can get the sense that your manifestation device and its chakra system really is a marvelous system of divine engineering.

Unfortunately, we do not all have fully functional chakra systems. In many cases our systems are either handicapped at birth, disabled as part of the socialization process in our dominant yang societies, or distorted as a result of an improper understanding of the nature and right expression of chakra energies. Two basic problems can lead to dysfunctional or distorted chakras. On the one hand, chakras can be damaged and blocked because of emotional, physical, or spiritual trauma. **Blocked chakras** fail to express adequate amounts of creative energy. They are atrophied centers that provide only the minimal energetic expression to ensure bodily survival and nothing more. **Damaged chakras** often express energy in negative or self-destructive ways. Chakras are very powerful and if you have a choice in the matter, you are far better off closing your chakras rather than leaving them open to draw and express energy negatively.

The other way that chakras can become dysfunctional is when there is no local energy available for triggering them. Remember your chakras are vortexes. They draw, focus, and shape the energy of creation in order to provide your body with its amazing creative powers. However, they cannot draw and focus energy if it is not available and under certain conditions, certain types of energy are not available.

You already have enough information to be able to understand this process. As you will recall, the energy of creation exists as a balanced duality with a potential polarity. The two basic polarities are yin and yang. Now consider this. Your chakras all draw from the unified pool of creative energy. However, they do not draw from the same polarity. Some of your chakras draw primarily yin, and others draw primarily yang. Your chakras cannot function properly if energy of the proper polarity is not available to them.

Now in your chakra system, the bottom three chakras are yang chakras. These chakras express your personal power, your ability to impose your intent on creation (third chakra), your ability to draw down the universal pool of energy and use it to manifest (second chakra), and your ability to ground that creation in physicality (root chakra). If you think about it, these lower chakras are characteristically masculine or yang based. They draw from the available yang in order to function.

On the other hand, your top three chakras are yin based. They provide you with your intuitive (third eye) powers, expressive (throat) abilities, and your connection back into the spirit world (crown chakra.). If you think about it, these chakras are characteristically yin and they draw from the available yin energy in order to operate and manifest.

The dual nature of your bodily energy system is captured symbolically by the Star of David (see Figure below). The star, which represents an empowered human (not coincidentally was this used as a mark of execution during WWII), symbolically expresses the balanced union of the higher chakra system (the top three chakras) and the lower chakra system (the bottom three) in an energetic system *controlled* by the heart chakra. In the Star of David, the upward pointing triangle represents the top three chakras and the bottom pointing triangle, the lower three chakras. When all chakras are fully functional and in balance, your light body or Merkaba is activated. You might also call this light body your God sphere and when it is finally activated, things get exciting for you.

Figure Seven: Merkaba and Light Body

Now you should have the picture. In situations where the energy of creation is balanced, the chakras easily work together and one side or the other goes out of balance only with great difficulty. However, under imbalanced energy conditions, difficulties begin to emerge. If, for example, you crank up the yang and crank down the yin, your lower bodily chakras will function beautifully and without much focused intent. However, your higher chakras will not have enough gas to operate. They will sputter, spark, and eventually atrophy for lack of available energy. They will never extinguish, of course, and you would be able to keep them operating if you tried hard. However, only the most dedicated spiritual aspirant would have the time and energy necessary to attain full functionality when yin is very weak.

Now you will understand why we say that when energy conditions are out of balance, you become disconnected. When we turn up the yang side of the energetic pool too much, your higher bodily chakras, the ones that give your body its intuition and its connection to the higher spiritual realms, shut down. You become disconnected from your own knowledge and disconnected from the higher realms. As we will see in our next section, this disconnection was an important feature of our second ascension attempt we all know by the name of Atlantis.

Atlantis

Keeping in mind your body's energy system, you now understand that in Lemuria the balance of yin/yang, while not totally equitable, was not enough to deactivate the higher chakras. As a result, balanced activation of the Merkaba was unproblematic. Unfortunately, we could not achieve ascension so we had to try again.

The main difference between Atlantis and Lemuria was, of course, the energetic balance. In Atlantis, we had to pump up the yang even more than in Lemuria. For the sake of visualization, we might say we increased the balance of the yang energy from thirty-five percent to fifty percent.

The extra yang had an immediate effect on the way our intent was manifested in physicality. With the rebalancing, our creative thoughts burst into physicality much faster than under Lemurian conditions. The evolution of the natural world and humanoid societies moved apace and much more was accomplished within much shorter periods. We built civilizations, developed technologies, and pursued the arts and sciences in a very vigorous and aggressive manner. Atlantis was a time of grand empires and sprawling cities. The history of the Atlanteans unfolded as the grand dramas of kings and queens.

As you might expect, under these new conditions, and with the new balance of energy, considerable momentum was generated in physicality. The level of "atomic excitation" grew steadily and we rapidly built up the momentum necessary to successfully traverse the quantum boundary. Everything looked great in fact except for one tiny little problem. Because of the profound energetic imbalance and the lack of yin energy, our connection to Spirit was totally severed. Our higher chakras did not fully activate as part of the maturation process of the physical body. As a result, virtually every Atlantean citizen drove their physical vehicle (body) around unaware of the higher realities and disconnected from their higher selves.

This profound spiritual disconnection made Atlantean civilization quite different from Lemurian civilization and many things happened in Atlantis that would have been inconceivable in Lemuria. Atlantis was very yang oriented. It was very expansive, conquest driven, and control based. Very little of the subtle spirituality and intuitive sensibility that arises from higher chakra activation existed. Atlanteans were often cold, callous, boorish, individualistic heathens. Of course, we should not judge since this was not their Spirit but their body. Their body functioned in an isolated fashion cut off from Spirit. We would say the body was controlled by the limited ego not aware of its purpose, not aware that it was Immortal Spirit, and not aware of the higher spiritual realities. It is difficult to find the right words to describe this but if you want a better idea at what a disconnected Atlantean might look like and act like, just look around you. Better yet, take a close look at yourself.

We, as Immortal Spirit, never believed that there would be a problem with this disconnection. We initially thought that when the time came for The Ascension and yin started to flood into this reality to rebalance the energy, we would be able to restore the connection by sending messengers into physicality to teach everyone about the true nature of their reality. The messengers would simply tell everyone that ascension was at hand, explain the nature of their energetic systems, and help activate the higher chakras. We naively thought that as the messengers told everyone the Good News (i.e., that they were not isolated egos), and as the higher chakras were awakened by the influx of yin, all the bodies in physicality would recognize the power and glory of their higher selves, welcome themselves into physicality, and sit back and enjoy the ride back up the Tree of Life.

Unfortunately, this scenario never actualized. Because the connection was so weak to begin with, we lost control of our manifestations to the little ego. Why? It turns out the ego is easily frightened. As the top three chakras started to dance with the new yin, connections to Spirit started to activate. As the higher spiritual realms where opened to the limited ego, it became terrified. It had lived in individuality, negativity, and isolation for so long that the glorious worlds of higher consciousness that began to open up to it drove it mad with fear, paranoia and what it thought was its own profound insignificance. As most often happens when the body is in fear, it lashed out in anger. It began to destroy the world. Out of fear, it rained down death and destruction on itself and others.

At first, this destruction was the sort of mundane destruction (i.e., war) we are all so familiar with in this world. However, this was only the start. Things got quite ugly as the higher chakras continued to energize. As the Atlanteans began manifesting with the power of all their chakras, all the negativity and self-destructiveness of the small Atlantean ego burst into physicality. They found awesome and terrible ways to express their self-destructive intent. The food system collapsed, all sorts of new diseases emerged, and horrible death spread out across the land. All this and more simply because the limited ego was frightened by its true glory.

As you know the story of Atlantis did not have a happy ending. In fact, it got so bad that we, as Immortal Spirit, finally had to euthanize the Atlantean bodies. It was either that or watch them find ever more horrible ways to kill themselves and their fellow citizens. To end our Atlantean experiment, Immortal Spirit turned an asteroid into the earth and that was that for our second ascension attempt.

Conclusion

In this chapter, we continued our story of The Ascension by examining in more detail our past attempts to raise the physical universe up through the quantum boundary. We learned our first attempt, Lemuria, did not generate the required energy for ascension. The reason for this was simply because there was not enough of the energetic yang to get the job done. We did note, however, that the Lemurian experiment was a grand success in terms of the quality of creation. Lemurians existed in a utopian world of balance, beauty and brilliance that to this day remains the dominant expression of Spirit in this universe (i.e., on other planets).

We also learned that our second attempt, Atlantis, was a completely different experience. Although we started with the same physical infrastructure, the energetic balance we worked with was far more skewed. This imbalance was immediately noticeable and, in the long run, uncontrollable. Matter, as it developed consciousness, never reconnected with its spiritual source. Our physical bodies and our egos did however reconnect with the power of the chakra systems. As the energy was rebalanced and the poor egos could not integrate everything that was happening to them, a terrible darkness spread over the land and Atlantis was destroyed.

Never wanting to throw in the towel, we decided we would make a third attempt. It is to an examination of this third attempt that we now turn.

CHAPTER FOUR:
OUR WORLD

Any sufficiently advanced technology
is indistinguishable from magic.

Arthur C. Clarke

Introduction

In the last chapter, we discussed in detail how we, as immortal Spirit, have attempted to create the conditions necessary for the ascension process. We discussed both Lemuria and Atlantis as failed attempts to break through the boundary and lift physicality back up the Ladder of Creation. Atlantis, we learned, was a huge disaster. Ironically, we are all still dealing with fallout from the Atlantean fiasco.

In this chapter, we are going to examine our current attempt at breaking through the boundary. As we will see, although the premise of the experiment is the same as the previous two experiments, and the energetic balance is identical to the Atlantean experience, the conditions of its unfolding are far more complex and difficult than previous attempts. Not only do we have the energetic fallout of Atlantis to deal with but we also had to be certain that when the time came to awaken the higher chakras, should the body get scared, it would not be able to wield the same destructive power as it had during the disintegration of Atlantis. However, before we get into the details of this attempt it is necessary, once again, to take a closer look at how energy works.

Energy Revisited – Entropy and Darkness/ Creation and Light

As noted above, in addition to having to navigate an ascension attempt, we also have the energetic fallout or "karma" of Atlantis to deal with. In order to understand what this means, and in order to understand why this attempt was so complex and difficult to organize, we need to consider and keep in mind three features of energy that have an impact on how we create. These qualities of energy are its persistence, neutrality, and valence.

We have already spoken about the persistence of energy. To say that energy is persistent is really just another way of talking about energy's inertia or momentum. You will recall from previous chapters that once you draw energy to yourself through intent, and once that intent is manifested or expressed, that manifestation tends to stick. You may want to think of energy and its manifestations as being viscous. Of course, the lower the vibration of energy (i.e., the lower you are in the dimensional fabric of the universe), the more viscous that energy is. This feature of energy is nicely illustrated by liquids such as oil or molasses that become thicker as the vibrational rate of the molecules slow.

Another important feature of the energy of creation is that it is neutral. Energy is just energy and it is morally and ethically inert. Energy makes no judgments about its use or abuse. It simply is. If you have difficulty with this concept, think of your own storage and use of energy. You eat food that is converted to energy that your body uses in activity. However, what you eat and how your energy is stored does not dictate what actions you might engage in. You and your body are always free to choose how to utilize stored food energy. You could sit and watch television, go running, or play with your children. The point here is that you have a choice and nothing prevents you from being an unhealthy couch potato with a high risk of heart attack or stroke if that is what you choose.

It is the same with the energy of creation. It is just energy and it does not care what you do with it. It has no mind, no will, and no morality. It is the substance of God, to be sure, but the energy in raw form is empty of Spirit and responds only to intent. As with your choice of activity, you have a choice on how you use this energy. You could take the amazing and wondrous gift that is the energy of creation and, for example, manifest a world of peace, justice, love and prosperity. On the other hand you could, if you so choose, take the gift and make everyone and even the world herself (mother nature) your enemy. In the end, it is your choice.

In addition to persistence and neutrality, energy also has what we might call valence. Valence means that energy carries a sort of qualitative imprint. This imprint is given to energy by your physical body. Remember, our bodies are manifestation devices and when fully activated they are very powerful conduits. As energy passes through your bodies, it takes on an imprint provided by your body's current emotional state.

The valence given to energy as it passes through your body can be described in a couple of ways. We can describe the valence in terms of its spin and its color. Your body can spin energy in one of two directions. You can spin it in a "clockwise" direction or in a "counterclockwise" direction. If energy is spun "clockwise," the energy manifests towards unity and integration. If the energy is spun "counterclockwise," the energy manifests towards disunity and disintegration. Not surprisingly, there is a relationship between energetic balance (yin/yang) and spin. If you turn up the yang or

87

energetic side, the conflict and strife engendered by the out of balance yang makes it easier to spin energy towards disintegration.

Energy can also have color. Color, as we use the term here, refers to emotional color and like spin it is something that is stamped onto energy as it passes through your body. Your body, which has a wide variety of possible emotional responses to stimuli, can impart a variable cornucopia of "color" onto the energy of creation. You can color energy with love, compassion, hate, jealousy, anger, etc. Whatever you can feel, you can stamp. Indeed, whatever you feel, you do stamp.

Now, combine the qualities of persistence, neutrality, and valence and you have a set of energetic qualities with profound implications. Because energy is neutral, you can draw it and choose to manifest whatever you like. Because energy has valence, you stamp that energy with your own personal imprint. Finally, because energy is persistent, what you manifest and how you manifested it sticks around. If you stamp energy with dark emotions, the energy you have used to manifest stays like that until you make a conscious effort to re-stamp it.

You can see that at root we are still talking about energetic inertia. However, now we have refined our understanding of what this inertia means and can now see that it includes not only the inertia of movement but also the inertia of color and spin. Let us now turn to an examination of the full implications of energetic inertia.

The Original Spin

One rather important implication of energetic inertia is that as you stamp and spin energy, the energy sticks around in that form in the general area where it was drawn. This energy then becomes available to others for their manifestation requirements. The problem here occurs because your body tends towards **sympathetic vibration**. It works like this. Your body draws energy to accomplish certain manifestation tasks.

If it draws neutral energy (unspun, uncolored) through its chakras, nothing untoward happens. However, if it draws energy with a valence, your body tends to react to that valence. For example, if there is a lot of angry energy floating around, and you just happen to be in the neighborhood of that angry energy, your creative efforts will draw from that energy first and as you try and manifest, your body will have a tendency towards anger. There is nothing mystical here. This is a simple physical reaction to energy.

Normally, energetic valence and sympathetic vibration are not significant problems for us. When we are fully conscious of who we really are, that is, when we remember we are Immortal Spirit, we would rarely spin or color energy in any negative fashion. If we did, we would be sure to re-imprint it as soon as possible to prevent energetic escalations. In turn, if we experienced someone else's improperly stamped energy, we would recognize it for what it was, take responsibility for it, and quickly *transmute* it into something more appropriate. There is no doubt we would do these things because as Spirit, we understand the full implications of leaving dirty energy around. This is simple energetic hygiene.

However, turn up the yang side and starve the higher chakras so that a veil (The Veil) is placed between the ego and the immortal self and the danger is that things can get out of control. When in amnesia, and when dealing with the excitations of the out of balance yang energy (think how difficult it is to remain calm on six cups of coffee), it becomes very easy for the body to simply react without thought to whatever energy happens to be available. If there is lots of energy stamped with negativity, the body feeds off that and becomes unpredictable. Consider a simple event like being cut off in traffic. There are wide ranges of reactions to this event and how we react will very much depend on a) the type of mood we are already in, b) what type of energy your body draws and c) how aware you are of your visceral bodily reactions. If we draw negative energy, and are not aware the energy *may not be our own* we can over react. Here arises the phenomenon of road rage.

You can see this dynamic clearly in crowd situations where panic or anger are contagious and where an initial event can cause an emotional ripple that cascades through the crowd and erupts into chaotic manifestation. You also see this principle operating, at a bit higher level, when you look at parts of the world that seem to be always full of conflict. This conflict is present because the individuals are working with heavily imprinted energy. Because the energy in these areas is so negatively spun and colored, manifesting anything positive becomes very difficult.

As noted, as Immortal Spirit, we would never over react to anything. In fact, when aware of our origins, it would be very unlikely that we would ever react in anger to anyone no matter what they had done. In addition, it would be inconceivable that we would spin energy in a negative fashion and forget to correct that mistake. However, in the body and in amnesia things are quite different. We forget who we are, forget who our sisters and brothers are, react inappropriately, spin energy in a negative direction, and forget we need to fix it. This is a significant problem for us on this earth where long ago in Atlantis we, in our ignorance and superstition, began imparting and reinforcing negative spin and valence. We might call the original energetic imprints that occurred as Atlantis spiraled into oblivion the *Original Spin*.

Once you have participated in the original spin, and when you are in amnesia, the real difficulties begin. While in amnesia, the negative spin that you have manifested makes it more likely that future manifestations by you or anyone else will take on the character of the imprinted energy. Given the right conditions, things can easily get out of control even in your current life setups. Consider what would happen while in amnesia, with your chakras wide open, and while you are reacting in absolute terror to your true spiritual heritage and you will have a better understanding of just how terrible the Atlantean descent into oblivion really was.

The One Law

As you can now understand, when things got ugly in Atlantis, negative imprinting literally gushed dirty energy into this area of physicality. What is important to understand here is that when we reconfigured this area to try to raise physicality up to the ascension barrier again, we were stuck with the energy stamped by the Atlanteans. All the anti-energy we generated in the descent hung around like a pool of mud and darkness in this area of the space/time tube.

This was a problem that we had to deal with. Even if we wanted to, which we did not, we could not just leave all this negative energy. Not only would it prevent our ascension attempt (we could never allow ascension to a higher vibratory dimension with all the negatively stamped energy kicking around), but all of those who participated in Atlantis were spiritually responsible for it. As Immortal Spirit, you are simply not allowed to muck around with energy, make your mistakes with it, and leave it for someone else to clean. As co-creators of physicality and partners in creation, we are all bound by the same universal spiritual law. This law operates as a sort of guaranteed balance mechanism and states that whatever you manifest, you must deal with. This is the law of spiritual responsibility or the One Law of the universe – so called because it is the only law we are a subject of.

The simplest way to describe the operation of this law is to say that it functions by returning to you any energy you stamp. If you stamp energy with goodness and manifest with this energy, this is returned to you in equal measure next time you need energy. If you stamp bad things onto energy, this energy is also returned to you in equal measure. This law returns to you the same quality energy you send and is an absolute law. There are no dispensations ever given and only out of ignorance would anyone want to continuously stamp energy with negativity. The anti-creative spiral they would find themselves locked into would lead to considerable pain and anguish and would become harder and harder to deal with as time passed and as the soul's available energy became increasingly negative.

As Spirit, we understand this law and can actually see it in immediate operation while in manifestation in the higher dimensions. In higher dimensions, the responsiveness of energy and its fluidity ensures a quick return on our energetic investment. Because of this "in your face" character, we are careful what we manifest. However, in lower dimensions and in amnesia, we can forget the operation of this law. In the lower dimensions, you can imprint energy and only reap what you have sown several years later. This lengthy disconnection between intent and return makes the operation of the One Law difficult to discern and is one of the reasons for all the misconception around this law.[13] Let us take a moment to clear up some of the misunderstandings of this law.

---

[13] Not that there are not ongoing efforts to remind you. This law is expressed in every world religion or spiritual belief system as some variant of the **Golden Rule**.

> Be' not deceived; God is not mocked: for whatsoever a man soweth, that shall he also reap. Galatians 6:7.

> All things whatsoever ye would that men should do to you, do ye even so to them: for this is the Law and the Prophets. Mathew 7:12.

Obviously, this is not a law of retribution. Although some might think you are given the OK by this law to go and pluck out an eye for an eye, it is not so. That particular interpretation is pure nonsense and violates the nature and intent of law. Not only does plucking out eyes ignore the fact that we are dealing with *energy* and not actions, but it also ignores the synergistic effect of fighting fire with fire. If you imprint negative energy with more negative energy, you simply get more negativity. If you fight fire with fire, you only get a bigger fire. If somebody hits you and you turn around and smack her or him back, you have generated twice the negativity that existed before. If you do this, you are in rank violation of this simple spiritual precept. A discerning person attentive to the One Law does not contribute to negativity but turns the other cheek.

What is hateful to you, do not to your fellowmen.
That is the entire law; all the rest is commentary."
Shabbat 31. Talmud.

This is the sum of duty: Do naught unto others which
would cause you pain if done to you. Mahabharata 5,
1517.

Hurt not others in ways that you yourself would find
hurtful. Buddhism. Udana Varga 5, 18.

Surely it is the maxim of loving-kindness: Do not unto
others that you would not have done unto you.
Confuscious Analects 15, 23.

That nature alone is good which refrains from doing
unto another whatsoever is not good for itself.
Zoroastrians: Dadistan-I-dinik, 94.

This list taken from http://users.aol.com/psyeditor/goldrule.html
and also http://www.teachingvalues.com/goldenrule.html

This is also not a law of judgment. As we have already discussed, there is no judgment implied in the use of energy. Let me repeat that. There is no judgment implied in the use of energy. Even the death of another person is not a negative event in and of itself. It is simply the end of the physical body. What is bad about it is the extent to which the people involved have to deal with some powerfully negative energetic imprints. When somebody kills someone, in addition to those left behind, you should also weep for the murderer because the depth of negativity and disconnection that is required to kill another being is so great that the murderer who has participated in the imprinting will require many lifetimes of carefully orchestrated cleanup work before the energy they are responsible for is clean.

To repeat, the One Law is not about retribution or punishment. The One Law is simply about responsibility. If you create something, it is your responsibility to deal with it. If you mess something up, you have to fix it. Although some may balk at this law, frankly this is the way of spiritual adulthood. You clean up after children. Adults fix their own messes.

Transmuting Energy

Now this brings us to the second reason why we incarnate on this earth. Remember the first reason is that we are ascension energy workers. In addition to being ascension workers, we are also cosmic janitors working to clean and shine all the energy that we stamped in our mad dash to oblivion in Atlantis. We call our energetic cleanup work transmuting energy and we are doing it in part because of the way the One Law operates. Although the job has been quite onerous, it is conceptually simple to undertake. All we have to do is take the energy into our bodies and send it back out through the appropriate chakras as something (anything) more positive.

Now although this is conceptually easy to understand, in practice it is very difficult. The body's own propensity for sympathetic vibration and its profound spiritual amnesia means that we have a strong tendency to *experience* the energy that we are seeking to transmute in a very bodily fashion. In other words, when any angry energy passes through our body, we get angry. Under these conditions, it is very difficult to remain detached from that anger and do our job. Instead, we have tended (especially in our initial incarnations) to simply pass that anger through in the same form and lash out at whatever kind soul triggered the angry expression. Those of us who have ever experienced powerful emotions (and since we are all energetic cleansers, we have all experienced powerful emotions) know just how difficult it is to turn this around. You must constantly struggle against the tide. In some cases, as with the energy spun in a counterclockwise direction and manifested as depression or self-destructiveness, it requires an individual to literally hit bottom before they finally step onto The Path and begin the incredibly difficult task of transmuting the energy.

Now you might ask at this point why we do not simply transmute the energy from the outside of physicality. That is, why do we not allow our higher selves (our souls, the angels, the archangels, the ascended masters, etc.) to collect all that energy and spin it away with love and light while we gaze in bliss at the space/time tube? Why do we insist on entering the body, falling into amnesia, and doing it the hard way. The reason is simple. Outside of the body, we only experience love. It is the physical body with its neurons, synapses, and senses that provides us with the rich emotional experience we have come to treasure. While we are not in body, we cannot feel all the energy that has been manifested on this earth. We can see the energy and its color and spin, of course, and we can adjust the energetic balance (and even "reboot" the area if we wish), however, outside of the body, we are helpless to change a

95

particular energetic stamp. We can only change what has been done by the body while in the body.

Karma and your Guide Network

To recap, because of the operation of the One Law, we must deal with the energy we stamp. Because of the physical properties of energy, once it is manifested in physicality by a body, we must deal with the negativity by entering a physical body.

The task of energetic cleansing has been quite difficult for us. Fortunately, we have not had to undertake our janitorial work alone. We do not simply enter into manifestation, begin creating our life circumstances, and start transmuting energy. It does not work that way. Not only would that be too difficult (and very likely to fail), but the stakes here (ascension) are too high and there are too many interested souls. As a result, we are provided with help and lots of it. Just how much help we have may surprise you.

All the help you get with your karmic tasks begins with a contract. Before you enter into manifestation on this earth, you sign a contract. This contract, called your karmic contract, specifies exactly the types of energetic work you will be expected to undertake during your incarnation, what sorts of help you can expect to receive, and what sorts of activities you will engage in.

This contract is made between you and your guide network. Your guide network consists of between two and five (sometimes more) souls who have some sort of connection to you. They may have been related to you in previous lives, may have been family in this life, or may volunteer to help for reasons of their own (they of course cannot help unless you allow them to). Once you sign your contract with these individuals, it is these disincarnate guides who become responsible for administrating your karma.

Once you incarnate, your guide network assists in manifesting situations that provide you with the opportunities you need to transmute a particular type of negative energy into a more positive valence. You of course agree to whatever is in the contract. You are not forced to do anything. However, once this contract is agreed to, and you descend into manifestation, you are bound to this contract and are not allowed to break out of it.

You might wonder why such a seemingly authoritative set of circumstances is required. The reason is simply that while in amnesia, and while you are disconnected from your higher self, you may have bouts of spiritual irresponsibility. You may chaff and champ at the karmic contract and whine and whittle away your days running away from your "destiny" so to speak. As noted above, while fully aware of your true nature, you would never shirk your spiritual responsibility. However, in amnesia it happens all the time. To avoid problems like interfering with your free will, the contract simply allows your guide network to work at manifesting situations that offer you, in love, repeated opportunities to transmute the energy you agreed to transmute whether your body likes it or not. This way, no matter how you might cry in your body, you will never be freed from your contract simply because it is something you agreed to while in possession of your full spiritual faculties.

As noted, your guides manifest situations that give you opportunities to re-stamp energy. If you have agreed to deal with anger, for example, you will find, especially in your early years, that anger will be a dominant feature of your surroundings. Anger will continue to dominate your relationships and life events until you successfully deal with your share of the negative valence. Once you do that, your karma is cleared and you may move on either to additional karmic tasks or higher spiritual work.

The situations that trigger your karmic opportunities are numerous and varied. However, the kind of life you have and the types of experiences you get as opportunities are left totally up to you in ongoing consultation with your guide network. For the most part you are unaware of the unfolding of karma in your life although you can become aware of it should you progress on the spiritual path. You can also see it (if you are watching) every time you repeat the same emotional struggle or conflict. The older you get, and the more failed opportunities you have had to clear negative energy, the more obvious the cyclical nature of your karmic cleansing opportunities become. Eventually, you will be literally pulling your hair out wondering why the same thing keeps happening to you over and over and over again.

Now you know why.

You also now understand why you repeatedly hear that there are no accidents. All situations in your life are manifested with the intent of clearing energy.

I will have more to say about karma and clearing your contracts (i.e., fulfilling your energetic obligations) in a subsequent chapter. For now you should understand that although the energetic cleanup has been a tough slog, we have won the day. At the time of this writing we have succeeded in re-imprinting almost all the negative energy that has ever been imprinted onto this area of physicality. Any energy being negatively imprinted at this point is being directed towards the accomplishment of some higher spiritual goals. Once this work is done, anything left over will be rapidly cleared or moved to quarantine locations where those who need to continue with energetic cleanup work will be given the opportunities they need to complete their karmic contracts. When that is finally done all we will have left is pristine, positive and properly balanced energy to work with. However, we are again getting ahead of ourselves.

Keeping the Spin Controlled - Introducing the Off Worlders

At the start of this chapter, we noted that this particular ascension attempt, although energetically equivalent to previous attempts (i.e., yin/yang balance), required a more complicated setup. The problem of energetic valence, the need for karmic contracts to deal with the fallout from Atlantis, and the existence of a veritable army of disincarnate guides gives you a good overview of about half the complications.

The other and stranger half of our ascension setup involves a complicated intergalactic intervention designed to keep you from accessing the full power of your bodily energy system until you had demonstrated your ability to successfully reconnect your higher chakras. Remember the mess that was left after Atlantis collapsed? We simply could not allow an amnesiac body to get anywhere near full activation of their bodily systems unless we were sure that they would be able to pass through the fear that inevitably emerged when reconnection of the higher chakras began.

This need to spiritually castrate all of you left us with a peculiar problem. We needed you to enter the body and do your work, but we needed to prevent you from accessing your full power so that we could avoid another Atlantean excess. Given the limitations that Immortal Spirit experiences when working with physicality from the outside, this castration could only be accomplished by monads in body. Now while we understood what we needed to do to prevent your access to power, getting somebody to put you into bondage was problematic. A body living with its higher self ensconced firmly in the seat of consciousness would never do such a horrid thing. Even if we could find a conscious being to do this, they could never accomplish their task with any degree of efficiency. They would always be releasing people from their bondage or teaching them the way forward even when it was not time.

What we needed was another group of amnesiac bodies cut off from their higher selves. Only a spiritually alienated race would undertake such an onerous and unpalatable task as binding its own brothers and sisters.

We created this race with an elegant cosmic intervention. What we did was alter the conditions of life on planetary systems close by this earth in order to create and evolve a race of intergalactic chakra administrators. We created our race of administrators by modifying the physical and energetic conditions on selected worlds in such a way as to foster the rise of a race of beings whose primary *raison d'etre* would be complete and utter control of their lived world. We did this by creating conditions that required this control in order for even basic survival. Although the details of this are quite complex, at heart all we did was create a planetary sphere characterized by lack of natural resources but an abundance of life. By putting living conditions out of balance in this fashion, we created a global struggle for existence and a world were competition and conflict were the main features of existence.

As a result of the fierce competitive struggle we fostered on these planets, no individual life form could survive without evolving a rather despicable set of characteristics. It was quite an interesting process really. In the lower life forms, natural selection gradually and inexorably selected the strongest, most aggressive, most violent, and most manipulative members of any given species. Each species evolved into a perfect Machiavellian diamond. Each species preyed on all others and as the traits of aggression, violence, and strength continued to be selected and refined, natural conditions became almost unbearably violent and competitive. This competitive environment was the ugly stage upon which the higher bodily forms could evolve.

As the higher life forms evolved on these planets, they also had to develop the same competitive and aggressive characteristics if they were to be able to successfully compete for the narrow and constantly changing ecological niches on their home worlds. However, it is in the development of their higher facilities (i.e., intellectual and emotional capabilities) that we find the most interesting, and most desired results. In terms of their emotional development, these beings were quite perverse and outside the normal evolutionary outcomes of this universe. They were emotionally stunted! Indeed, they lost the capacity to feel quite early in their development. The reason for the emotionally stunted quality of their evolution is simple. Feelings got in the way of their survival. Sentiment of any sort was a weakness. Even emotions like anger or hatred did no good because they interfered with basic survival responses during their biological and social evolution. After all, it was not the angriest competitor who won a place in the ecological niche (or the competitive hierarchies they developed) but the one most able to adapt and find opponent weaknesses.

Putting their stunted emotional development another way, we might say that conditions on their planet encouraged the atrophy of their heart chakra. By the end of their evolutionary development, these beings had very small heart centers. Their small physical hearts (a result of their chakra atrophy) could support only very tiny physical forms. This atrophy of the heart chakra was critical in the plan of Spirit to control your manifestation powers in the third ascension attempt. Without a functioning heart chakra, our race of, let us call them "Grays," could not spin or color energy. Without functioning heart chakras, they could not ever participate in any energy debacle. This was as planned. We did not want them causing the same energy fiasco we all experienced in Atlantis.

As their bodies shrunk and their hearts dwindled, you would have thought that they would have perished on their competitive worlds. However, they did not. They thrived. The only reason they ended up being survival candidates on their own world was that their intellectual facilities were overdeveloped. Because of the harsh conditions, and because sentiment had been selected out of them so early on, the energy for their evolution went straight to their intellect. They became highly intelligent and rational – almost perfectly so.

Of course, the goal of their thinking processes was always control. In fact, their propensity to control was, of all the traits that had been designed into their bodies by Immortal Spirit, the most perfectly developed by the evolutionary process. The horrific environments they lived in demanded that they get control. If they could not get control of their environments, they would forever be flailing on the food chain and no advanced social development would be possible. As the heart atrophied and their intellectual capacity grew, so too did their desire for control. Control of their lived world eventually became for them the only reason for their existence. Because control led to their ability to survive and furnish, it was honored above all other traits. In the end, they became beings of almost perfect instrumentality. They never did anything out of passion, anger, love, or kindness. They always did things to further control of their environment.

Their inbred desire for control was expressed in their social, political, and technological systems. Their social and political systems elevated rational thought, competition, strength, struggle, and control as the highest values of life. Those who could not compete or could not attain control over their lived world, and those who were weaker, were all unilaterally dismissed as unfit for survival or reward. It was not much better for those who could function in these intense social systems. Those who survived were simply pinned into ridged hierarchies based on pseudo scientific rationalizations of worth or ability with the strongest and brightest on top and in control and the weakest at the bottom and serving those above. Their society was a perfect bureaucracy. Our bureaucratic systems are but poor copies of the grandeur these beings achieved.

More interesting than their social and political systems was their philosophical and religious discourse. As religion melded with an emerging philosophy, and as they began to think about themselves and their position in the world they lived in, they developed a horrific outlook. They saw in creation a vile and despicable cosmos. When they considered the possibility of a God or Gods that had participated in the creation of the universe, they saw only madness. What pantheon, what God, they thought, would create such an atrocity as their world with its out of balance ecosystems, its constant upheaval, and its poor management? What God would create punishing living conditions where struggle and scarcity were the primary facts of life? At worst, some saw their God as a demented control freak sticking his creative fingers into primordial soups with the intent of creating life solely for the sake of torturing it. At best, some saw an instrumental God that played with the universe and created living conditions solely out of some twisted desire to experiment with life.

As this race of beings (actually there were several candidate planets) developed, we as Immortal Spirit, watched and aided their development. We encouraged them along their odd path. Their local spiritual hierarchy oversaw the entire process and helped those who had volunteered to live lives as these "dark forces" manifest the conditions that would encourage their evolution along agreed to lines. When a race finally became available that fulfilled the conditions we had set out, technology for space travel was introduced and we watched them quickly break the physical barriers that separated their species from the rest of this physical universe.

As they broke the barriers to interplanetary travel, they did exactly what we expected them to do. They sought to expand the material base of their civilization (i.e., expand their ecological niche) and went out to find worlds to control, dominate, and exploit. As they found technologically undeveloped and primitive planets, they placed the people of these planets into productive slavery (i.e., made them farmers, miners and workers) and siphoned off the wealth they generated for their own personal use. They found many worlds to dominate and to each one of these they came as bigheaded Gods with magical technology to dazzle the eyes of the unsophisticated denizens.

When the beings came to this planet, they finally had fulfilled their sacred mission. They enslaved you with their systems of control and in that enslavement they prevented you from accessing your vast spiritual power. They cut you off from your manifestation powers, stunted your chakra system, and left you in almost total spiritual, political, and social ignorance. In this state, there was virtually no possibility that you would ever get access to the power of your body. However, you would still be able to function as janitors because, unlike the Grays (also known as the Annunaki), you still had a heart.

The Grays accomplished their task with perfect precision. They kept you from your power and never once was the pain they inflicted upon you the outcome of any negativity or hatred they felt. They never took any pleasure in the tortures or slavery they submitted you to. They did their thing for purely instrumental reasons. Because of their lack of emotional response, they never once came close to creating another Atlantis. It was a beautiful outcome, the execution of which shines considerable glory on The One who instigated this whole ascension drama.

Of course, the enslavement was only to be temporary. It was written in the stars that our ascension attempt would eventually be successful. At that point, the intention was to call all of you (oppressor and oppressed) home to rejoin with each other as spiritual family in full consciousness.

Our plan went mostly as intended and the conditions for ascension were achieved in very good time. Indeed, the conditions for ascension were met some time ago. At that point, the call went out to the Grays and they began their return home. Unfortunately, as they began their return, they left control of this planet and control of the systems of slavery in the hands of humans. While the Grays pursued their own spiritual freedom, the humans they had left in control pursued your spiritual bondage. However, we are getting ahead of ourselves here. Let us turn now to a discussion of how the Grays found their way back to Spirit.

The Grays Return Home

The story of the Grays return to Spirit is an interesting one and it revolves around the key characteristics of these intergalactic administrators – their lack of emotion. As noted above, an atrophied heart chakra was an important characteristic because we did not wish these Grays to participate in another Atlantis. They had to find you and bind you for sure, but they would have to undertake their sacred task totally devoid of emotion.

Of course, the Grays understood that they were lacking in emotion. They could see it on all the worlds they conquered and they understood they lacked this curious mechanism. However, they never believed this to be a handicap. Ironically, they thought it gave them strength over others. They could see, for example, how easily sentiment and emotion could be turned against those they ruled. It was perfectly plain to them that emotional responses of any type detracted from the precision and rationality of a control strategy, thereby weakening it. They would use emotion as a way to strengthen their domination of others, but they never saw their lack as anything but a strength. Until, that is, they came into contact with advanced civilizations.

When the Grays first contacted civilizations more advanced then they, they expected these contacts to go much as their previous contacts had gone. They would find the weaknesses of the species, work to overcome them, and enslave the people. Unfortunately, things did not work out this way for them. Although they tried to control and dominate these advanced civilizations, they could **never** get the upper hand on them.

At first, our interplanetary administrators had a hard time understanding why they could not overcome these advanced worlds. They tried everything in their power. They copied technology, tried military force, and even attempted to weasel their way into positions of power and authority on those worlds that would adopt them. Yet no matter what advances they made, advanced civilizations always seemed to stay one step ahead of the feeble attempts of the Grays to get the upper hand.

Being the quintessential control freaks that these beings were, their inability to get control bothered them. It bothered them so much that finding out why they could not get the upper hand on these worlds became an obsession for them. Our story gets quite beautiful here because the reason they could not get the upper hand on these worlds was because they had severed their own emotional and spiritual connections eons back in their evolutionary process. Although they did not realize it at the time, when the Grays began working on the problem of control, they also began working on the problem of their own spiritual and emotional atrophy. Little did they know that their work on this problem would eventually lead them back into the loving arms of their higher selves and their own spiritual hierarchies.

The Grays initially conducted many investigations of a political, psychological, biological, and social character. At first, they had a hard time. They could see something was going on, but they could not determine why these civilizations were always able to stay one step ahead.

The reason for the Gray's inability to conquer these worlds was simple. The advanced civilizations all had fully functioning chakra systems and wide-open connections to the higher spiritual realms. It is hard to underestimate the significance of this. With fully open connections and fully functioning manifestation devices, beings have total access to the full creative force of Spirit. This creative force is unspeakably powerful and competent. Because of this, it was one thing for our Grays to conquer a primitive planet. It would always be impossible for them to conquer an advanced world. They simply could not compete against their own higher selves or the full force of Spirit.

At first, our Grays did not understand what they were seeing. However, as they turned more of their attention to the problem they eventually began to detect the subtler types of energies at work in the universe. This started them on a more focused search that led them to discover the energetic capabilities of physical bodies. As they finally realized the existence of this energetic system (the chakra system), their eyes widened in shock and they gasped in horror. Every other race, even the ones they conquered, had this system. However, they could they not see it in themselves!

The shock of this revelation that they had some sort of cosmic handicap that placed them beneath every other race of beings in the cosmos was so profound and so unsettling that for the first time in millennia they felt an emotion. Our Grays felt fear for they could not understand how in this entire universe only they did not have these amazing capabilities. If they had thought at one time of a mad God, now they feared a punishing God that had singled them out for some horrible eternal damnation.

Being quintessentially rational, they quickly overcame their superstitious fear. However, the realization of their uniqueness in this universe changed things for them. They lost all interest in conquering and controlling planets and they largely withdrew (though they did retain scientific interest) from the planets they had conquered and left them to those indigenous individuals who had helped them in their planetary domination. These people, the elites of your world, cut off from their overlords, simply continued the systems of domination (with more or less awareness of the original conditions and the original overlords) up to the end of the 21st century. Their story we tell in the next chapter.

As for the Grays, they only had one goal now. This was to find out what was wrong with them and why they had been so handicapped. They engaged in increasingly vigorous investigations of themselves and others in increasingly sophisticated attempts to understand why such a terrible cosmic joke had been played on them. Yet, for all their great intelligence it took them many thousands of years to finally realize what their particular problem was.

They could not experience emotions. They did not have a heart.

Well that is not quite true. They did have a heart, but it was small, atrophied, and not very good at drawing the energy associated with emotional expression. Failure to have an emotion meant they were unable to efficiently manifest using their chakra system and unable to activate their light body. Being unable to activate their light body meant they would never be able to conquer a civilization that could activate the Merkaba.

After overcoming some deep initial fear that perhaps they would never be able to experience emotions, they recalled from their not too distant past how, when they first realized their handicap, they had felt fear. Buoyed by this fact they set out to trace the evolutionary and biological sources of their own genetic limitations. They quickly realized how their own planetary conditions had selected emotional response out of them. They could also see how they themselves had reinforced that selection in their own philosophical, ideological, psychological, social, and political systems. Finally, they also saw what needed to be done to repair the problem and restore their atrophied emotional responses. All that was required was a little philosophical revision and a little cross species genetic diffusion.

This is the point where the Grays currently sit. Their realization of what they have been missing has only come in the last few hundred years and they are only now beginning their healing process. As they begin this process, they have also begun an incredibly beautiful and joyous reconnection to their Spiritual selves. As they awaken, they have finally learned what their true role in the ascension drama was and how they were created to fulfill a critical and sacred task. Many of these Grays (Annunaki) have even returned to this earth to help with the final ascension and awakening tasks. Many more have actually chosen to incarnate in the human body to experience what it has to offer and to share their knowledge with others who walk the path of awakening.

Now, despite the fact that the Grays did such an incredible job, and despite the fact that we are at the ascension point and ready to wake the entire earth up to the grand drama we have all participated in, there is resistance to turning the cosmic page. There are two problems here. One problem (the easier one) we have involves the pace and timing of awakening. Obviously, waking people up to this grand ascension drama has to be done carefully. Given the level of darkness and the profound disconnection that characterizes the bodies of this world, you simply could not send an emissary in and start yapping about energy, the ascension, slave masters, and karmic contracts without eliciting a violent, paranoid, and vengeful reaction. As you will recall this was part of the problem in Atlantis and nobody wanted a repeat of that. In this ascension attempt we have undertaken the awakening process in a very controlled, very gentle fashion.

Bringing this world to the point where we could gently awaken the sleepers of this world was one problem, but it was not the most intractable problem. We could have accomplished this awakening several thousand years ago if it was not for the fact that the rulers of this world did not wish to let you go.

Initially, resistance to the spiritual truth came from the Annunaki overlords. Until they had responded to their wake up call, they essentially ignored or destroyed any emissaries that came with the message to "let God's people go." However, as time passed and they started to focus on their own spiritual problems, and as they lost interest in this world, the resistance shifted from them to the human elites that had helped the Annunaki dominate the people of this planet and who were left in control as the Annunaki left this world. These human overlords continued with the prerogatives of the original Annunaki overlords and continued to keep the masses of this planet enslaved. They did not like the idea of releasing the people of this planet. A combination of their own fear and greed had (has) made them determined to retain their privileged positions. In fact, they have been so desperate to prevent the final day of reckoning that they have demonstrated they will go to just about any length to prevent a successful ascension and awakening process. They would even go as far as to destroy this world.

This has been a significant problem for us. As we will see in the next chapter we have had to engage in some pretty sophisticated interventions to get this world to the point where we could counter elite machinations and proceed with awakening and ascension in a relatively safe and non violent manner. It is only very recently, i.e., since the late '80s, when conditions in the space/time tube have improved to a point where this has become possible.

Conclusion

In this chapter, we covered significant spiritual ground. Here you were introduced to our most recent attempt at traversing the ascension boundary and some of the energetic complexities we have had to deal with because of the Atlantean debacle. You learned that although the universal pool of creation energy comes as a duality, the physical body is able to take that duality and stamp additional characteristics on that energy. As the Atlanteans rushed headlong into their own destruction, they left themselves and the many who came to help in this ascension attempt, with an energetic debt that, owing to the operation of the One Law, needed to be paid out.

In this chapter, you were also introduced to the Annunaki (Grays). As you learned, these heartless beings came to this world with the divinely sanctioned task of keeping you from manifesting your full creative power. This spiritual bondage you were placed into was necessary so as to avoid another Atlantean debacle. As we saw, the Annunaki were quite successful in their divine task. They even released you, as planned, after they responded to their spiritual call home. Unfortunately, we were not able to proceed to the awakening process because the human elites who had worked under the Annunaki took over when their former overlords left.

In the next two chapters, we will outline in some detail the spiritual interventions that were necessary to overcome the Machiavellian machinations of the elite hordes of this planet. As you will come to see, many volunteers came from many locations in the cosmos to help create the conditions that would allow the people of this planet to awaken so that The Ascension could finally proceed.

CHAPTER FIVE:
EMISSARIES OF LIGHT I

And it's whispered that soon
If we all call the tune
Then the piper will lead us to reason.
And a new day will dawn
For those who stand long
And the forests will echo with laughter.

Led Zeppelin, Stairway to Heaven

Introduction

By now, you have developed a comprehensive overview of The Ascension. You have learned of the nature of the process, the nature of our previous attempts, and the odd configuration of our most recent ascension effort. As we learned in the last chapter, the fallout from the destruction of Atlantis and the way in which the Atlanteans slammed themselves into oblivion required additional setup features. In addition to having to work towards The Ascension, we also had to work towards cleaning up the energetic debt left by the Atlantean debacle and we had to do it while our energy bodies were severely handicapped by the Annunaki planetary administrators.

Although profound, the spiritual slavery you were placed into by the Annunaki was supposed to be a temporary situation. The plan was that once you had achieved the spiritual goals of this third attempt, your slave masters would be called to awaken to their higher purpose, would release you from your bondage, and the entire 3D world (Annunaki included) would enjoy the incredible front row view of The Ascension. Unfortunately, we ran into a small snag. While the

113

conditions for ascension have been met, and while the original Annunaki successfully followed their awakening call and are now standing ready and willing to assist you with the process of spiritual awakening, we have experienced continued resistance from the earthly elites who benefited from the Annunaki systems of power, hierarchy, and privilege.

In this chapter and the next we will detail some of the starseed interventions that have been required in order to overcome ongoing efforts of this world's elites to prevent the ascension of physicality and the awakening of this planet's people.

The War of Souls

When you consider the fact that you have been ready for ascension on this planet for several thousand years, you get some sense of the frustration that we, as Immortal Spirit, have felt. We had paid our karmic debts and achieved energetic conditions for traversing the boundaries when pharaohs still walked this earth. Unfortunately, the elites who control this planet repeatedly refused to release the people of this earth from their social, psychological, and spiritual bondage and have instead worked diligently and tirelessly to prevent ascension and awakening.

This whole debacle with the world elites refusing to release you from your spiritual bondage started when we sent the first spiritual messengers into the space/time tube. They came to bring the Good News to the amnesiac bodies that they were part of higher spiritual realities and that the sort of experiences they had been having (e.g., death, poverty, famine, illness, etc.) where not a necessary component of their existence. The message that was repeatedly sent was **clear**. You had all volunteered to perform a wondrous sacred task, you had completed that task, and you were now free to return to Spirit and bring this world into full consciousness.

Unfortunately, the world elites (not nearly as bright as the Annunaki but far more vicious and spiteful) could not understand or appreciate the divine beauty of the message nor did they think ascension and awakening would be such a good idea. They did not welcome spiritual messengers coming into "their" world and telling them it was time to release the slaves they had worked so hard to oppress. In fact, they reacted quite badly to the idea and instead of looking at the awakening call as an opportunity to rejoin with their higher selves, they resisted, coveted their wealth and power, and became fearful of what would happen to them should the people of this earth experience a true kundalini activation. Having developed their own extremely vile and punitive legal systems, and thinking that these systems would be turned against them, they scrambled for **anything** that would prevent the loss of their own wealth and privilege.

As it turns out, stopping The Ascension and awakening was relatively easy for the world elites. They simply twisted the messages of the spiritual emissaries so that they became justifications for slavery instead of invitations to freedom. When the emissaries upped their pressure by sending more emissaries with more powerful messages, the elites reacted by clamping down even harder. They killed the messengers and oppressed those who followed them. When even that failed to turn back progress, the elites became frightened and desperate and in their desperation and paranoia they engaged in what we might call an energy gambit. They tried to turn the energy of ascension back by mucking up the energetic mix. In a strategy that duplicated the fiasco of Atlantis (but on a much smaller scale), they invoked war, famine, disease, and death in the hope that the populations of this earth would re-stamp enough energy with negative spin and color that Spirit would have to halt the awakening and return the bodies of this planet to their energetic cleanup work.

Turns out, sending the "Four Horsemen of the Apocalypse" (as the elites have called war, famine, disease and death in their own anti-ascension how-to manuals) worked. During the first few attempts the people of this earth, who had remained in a good degree of superstitious fear and paranoia under elite tutelage, followed the clarion call of war and destruction with little thought. They believed the elites when they said the enemy was "over there," that they were "evil" (and we were "good"), and that they had done horrible things.[14] At the behest of the world elites, "we" gleefully went out to kill anyone the elites said we should. As things got ugly and the energy started to turn dark with negativity, Spirit was indeed forced to call off ascension and the populations of this earth settled back into ignorance and slavery.

This strategy of the elites was a problem for Immortal Spirit. In order to counter it, Spirit sent additional teachers and healers to show people how to avoid war and see through the deception of the ruling elites. The hope was that these teachers and healers could heal the fear implanted by elites and teach people of their true spiritual heritage. The healers and teachers had a hard time of it though. They were often recognized as threats to the status quo and were immediately suppressed. When ascension and awakening was again attempted, the elites again reacted. They increased the oppression of the healers and teachers by torturing them, burning them as witches, and engaging in random acts of brutality to scare the populations. They stepped up their holy crusades of death and destruction, spread famine, and were once again successful in forcing the reversal of ascension.

---

[14] The debacle over the World Trade Center is the most recent expression of this centuries old strategy.

116

This back and forth spiritual struggle with the world elites has been going on a long time. Since our first attempt to awaken and ascend this planet many thousands of years ago, we have been engaged in what can only be called a War of Souls. As you can well imagine, it has been a difficult and frustrating struggle. Each time we tried to awaken the people of this planet and failed, we introduced new interventions. Each time we did that, the elites reacted with more brutality. However, as is the way with Spirit and creation, we made continual forward progress. With each failure, we learned more. With each new intervention, we got closer to ascension and closer to awakening.

And so we danced with the elites of this world for centuries in this grand War of Souls. It has been very much like a violent cosmic ping-pong game. As each awakening attempt grew increasingly successful, elite reaction grew increasingly violent and oppressive. In our most recent failed attempt (associated with WWII), we got so close to ascension and awakening, and the elites became so fearful and paranoid, that they raised a murderous darkness so vile and powerful that it threatened to destroy the entire world.

Although WWII was a very dark moment in the spiritual history of this planet, it was also the moment of greatest hope. Before that conflict we got so close to awakening that it was only the threat of world destruction that forced us to turn back. However, after the end of that conflict we, as Immortal Spirit, realized we had finally learned all we needed to know about the world elites. As a result, we were quite sure that our next awakening attempt would be successful.

At that point, a cosmic telephone call went out and everyone in the cosmos got very excited. Could it be that finally ascension and awakening was just around the corner? Would our next attempt be successful? The answer of course is yes. Our next attempt would be successful. In anticipation of this last attempt, we began our preparations for the final battle between the elites of this earth and Immortal Spirit. This final battle was long ago foretold in name as the Battle of Armageddon.

The Battle of Armageddon we have fought is a fantastic battle. The story is filled with tales of light and dark, oppressor and oppressed, magic, mysticism and mayhem. It is the story of beings of great light and beings of great darkness and the unfortunate return to essence of many who have refused to heed God's call. However, for all its darkness and violence, the Battle of Armageddon is also the beautiful story of awakening, reconnection, and glorification of Spirit in matter. Many people will tell this story in the coming years. For my part, I would like to spend some time outlining all the interventions that prepared the way for this final battle. In the remainder of this chapter and in the next I will speak of the historic starseed interventions and the creation of the glorious Infrastructure of Light which has made possible the initiation and successful completion of the Battle of Armageddon.

Let us start our examination by looking at the work of the ascended spiritual masters.

Ascended Masters

Let us start our discussion of ascended masters and starseed intervention by considering just what an ascended master is and the nature of their work on this planet. Consider first the word "master." This word has a very mundane meaning. A master is simply someone who is an acknowledged expert in any particular field of endeavor. Masters get to be masters because of their motivation and commitment to whatever it is they seek to be masters of. These individuals have trained, studied, trained, practiced, trained, and studied until they know their specialties so well that the expression of their creative intent becomes automatic and perfectly executed every time. Consider a master piano player (concert pianist), master carpenter, or master teacher for some idea of what being an accomplished master is all about.

Nothing special about a master.

Now, just like we can have master pianists and master teachers, we can also have masters in the ways of Spirit. In general, a spiritual master is someone who is so well versed in the ways of spirit, creative expression of divine will, and physicality that these individuals are able to teach, instruct and lead individuals towards ever greater expressions of divine will and consciousness. At least, this is the way of the spiritual master on most worlds. On this particular planet, and because of its sacred place in creation, a spiritual master would, in order to be called a master, have to have developed an additional set of skills and abilities. Spiritual masters here have to be conversant not only in the ways of consciousness but would also have to understand the limitations of consciousness in matter and how consciousness and our bodily energy systems have been distorted by world elites. They would need this knowledge in order to fulfill the task they came to fulfill which was to carefully lead the fragile and weak ego back towards a realization of its divine origin and purpose.

Nothing really special about spiritual masters either.

Now an Ascended Spiritual Master is simply a master with light body activated and eyes wide open. Let us call ascended spiritual masters spiritual emissaries to distinguish them from ascended masters in other disciplines. Spiritual emissaries are simply spiritual masters who are fully awake to their mission, have a fully functioning bodily energy system, and are thus in full possession of their creative powers.

119

As I noted above, spiritual emissaries have been a critical component of our ascension interventions. These individuals were the first ones to come to this planet and ask that people be freed from their bondage. They were also the first ones to die at the hands of the ruling elites for bringing such a message. They have been here since the beginning and have repeatedly entered into physicality after each failed ascension attempt. Of course, their work has changed over time as each awakening attempt failed, each new condition was added, and more starseeds came to participate in the grand War of Souls. However, their activity has always been guided by their one overriding goal, to help create an Infrastructure of Light that would provide an unshakeable foundation for ascension and awakening.

Just what is an Infrastructure of Light? It is the total of all the progressive spiritual, social, political, and psychological teachings that have been introduced to this world. It is the sum of all technologies that starseeds have brought to help raise the level of consciousness on this planet. In short, the Infrastructure of Light is the sum of all starseed intervention as it was directed at overcoming elite imposed darkness. The Infrastructure of Light is all around you and exists as the glorious manifested intent of millions of light workers. It is a truly magnificent edifice.

Spiritual emissaries had a very important role to play in the creation of this infrastructure. They came to introduce a critical sub-component of this edifice. They came to build the Spiritual Infrastructure of Light. This was a most dangerous job for two reasons. On the one hand, the truths they came with were very powerful truths that were easily recognized as spiritual truths and had a powerful tendency to "activate" people who were listening. Once a somnambulistic individual heard the uncorrupted truth as set out in the teachings of the spiritual emissaries, they were often rapidly set free from their spiritual bondage.

Because of the tendency for spiritual masters to free people from their spiritual bondage, they and the truths they brought were obvious threats to elite prerogative. As a result, the elites targeted the messages and the individuals who incarnated to bring them. Since elites, especially during the early centuries, had privileged access to the means of distributing truths (only priests could write, for example), twisting the truth and making the high spiritual knowledge of the emissaries into instruments of your spiritual bondage was quite easy. Of course, twisting the truth was never enough. Since the elites have always retained a monopoly on the use of force, murdering the emissaries and oppressing their followers when they needed to was never a problem either.

Never daunted, the spiritual emissaries continued to press truth into this reality. After considerable trial and error, spiritual emissaries modified their strategies and learned to hide the truth in innocuous places or to present the truth in multi-layered or coded messages. In the final version of their strategy for building the Infrastructure of Light, the spiritual emissaries even developed a brilliant way to get the elites themselves to help distribute the truth. They did this by creating structures of myth with multiple levels of meaning that, on the surface, could be turned into instruments of bondage but that retained, at the deepest level and hidden away from the understanding of the elites, powerful embedded truths that could be used to activate individuals through a process of spiritual revelation.

When these specially coded messages first started to appear, elites reacted in the same way they always did. They murdered the messengers and repressed their followers. However, as the elites twisted the spiritual messages into their own vile service, they found in these messages very powerful tools of bondage; more powerful in fact than they had ever seen. How brilliant was it, after all, to be able to teach the masses that spiritual advancement actually meant the sacrifice of the body to the elites of this world. With a great amount of self-satisfied glee, world elites proceeded to expend incredible effort distributing these coded spiritual message to all corners of the globe.

Of course, most people (elites included) could not see past the surface truths that were used as messages of bondage. However, this was part of the plan. Unlike previous awakening attempts, the point was not to wake people up instantly but to implant the coded messages in as many brains as possible so that when the time came, a massive population awakening could be triggered with elegant (but hidden) spiritual triggers. When the triggers were released (either to a single individual or as part of the collective awakening), individuals would very quickly awaken to the truth of their incarnation here and the true power of their energetic devices.

The elites performed the job of the emissaries admirably. In every culture, in every religion, on every continent, and in virtually every mind on this earth, the core metaphors and spiritual truths exist in some form. Now, this spiritual gunpowder just sits there, buried inside your head, waiting to be triggered. Once triggered, the awakening process is, considering the depth of darkness most of us have been forced to walk in, very rapid. This is not to say the process of awakening is an easy process. It is not. Awakening, as we will see in chapter seven, is a process of personal growth that can involve painful unblocking of energies. The whole process can also be very disconcerting because of its rapidity. Keep in mind the key to walking The Path quickly and safely is to trust Spirit.

Since the early sixties, Spirit has been awakening individual starseeds and light workers with individual triggers. These advanced cadres of light workers have been in operation now for almost two decades preparing the way for the explosive awakening that would be triggered during the proper divine moment. In 2001, the last of the specialist starseeds were activated. Beginning in 2003, the mass triggering has begun (you are reading this book, aren't you?). Now everyone is receiving triggers – no exclusions! As the divine fire is lit under every "body" on this planet, the next couple of years should prove very interesting.

The Ascended Master Support Network (AMSN)

Introducing the spiritual gunpowder described above was not an easy task. As noted, those who came to introduce high spiritual truths faced several problems. One difficulty was the outright hostility and violence of elite rulers. The elites of this world invariably identified any spiritual emissary with significant public exposure as a threat to the status quo. Once identified, ruling elites set out to tempt and divert the messengers from their mission, distort their teachings and murder the emissaries. Even a cursory glance at the history of authentic prophets, scientists, philosophers, and healers demonstrates the horrible fate that awaited those who chose to stand against ignorance and superstition. To this day, all those who hold positions outside the mainstream (the "mainstream" simply referring to a way of thinking and perceiving that is palatable to the ruling elites and supportive of the bondage you are subject to) run the risk of being exposed to ridicule, disgrace and ruin.

Another difficulty that hampered the work of the emissaries was the simple fact that all emissaries who came to assist with the awakening and ascension process began their missions in total amnesia. Of course, not all emissaries needed to return to full consciousness to fulfill their missions. Many of the emissaries, especially the ones who came with science, philosophy, technology, or the healing arts, were able to attain their objectives while participating in the darkness of this planet. However others, and especially the spiritual emissaries, needed to be fully awakened in order to accomplish their mission. These ones simply could not teach the spiritual truths they needed to teach while experiencing any degree of amnesia.

Unfortunately, even spiritual emissaries are not able to come into this world with fully functioning connections (i.e., with activated higher chakras). Just like you and me, they also work within an environment where the chakras are starved of energy. Although stronger than the average incarnated soul, they still work uphill against the deficit of yin.

This created a bit of a problem for us. We knew that, given the hostility of the ruling elites to progressive spiritual messages, our emissaries would probably not make it far along into their awakening process before they were identified as the political and spiritual threats they were, tempted off the mission path, or destroyed altogether. So in order to protect these individuals from temptation and destruction long enough for them to awaken to their task and fulfill their missions, a special support group of starseeds tasked with the job of protecting, nurturing, and supporting the spiritual emissaries was created. This support network we might call the Ascended Master Support Network (AMSN). The AMSN, also known as *mystery schools,*[15] consisted of a powerful network of incarnated and disincarnated spiritual guides. These guides (similar to your own guide network, but far more accomplished) provided the assistance and protection needed by the ascended masters so that they might be nurtured and returned to full consciousness.

Incarnated guides, i.e., those souls who came into the body to prepare the way for the spiritual emissaries, provided some of the initial training and protection required. However, because these incarnated

---

[15] The most famous, and most benign, of these schools today surround the Tibetan monks and their esoteric practices designed to rediscover the Dalai Lama after each round of death and reincarnation. Each time the Dalai Lama dies, the monks of this school set out on an amazing quest to find the next incarnation of this most holy individual. Once identified, the Dalai Lama is taken as a child and carefully brought back to full remembrance within the safe confines of the Tibetan monasteries.

In addition to training the ascended master each time he returns, this monastery complex also functions as spiritual havens for those stepping onto The Path.

guides were working in this world, they were subject to the same conditions as the ascended masters (i.e., temptation, persecution, death). As a result, they normally performed their tasks with some degree of amnesia (to prevent their exposure) and they normally performed only identification and initiatory functions. That is, they actively sought out ascended masters as they entered into incarnation (they identified them), they provided protection (sometimes physical, always spiritual) so they could grow in the awareness of their task, and they provided a minimal initial training (advice on the discipline of chakra activation, for example) so that spiritual emissaries could reconnect with their primary guide network (the disincarnated masters).

Clearly, the incarnated support workers had a limited function. They only needed to get the chela (master candidate) past a certain stage of spiritual development. Once the chela had begun the activation process, they would naturally turn to their disincarnate guide network where the remainder of their development was overseen. This approach of turning the chelas over to their disincarnate guides was the safest and most powerful way of returning them to full consciousness. Once even minimally reconnected, these individuals became immune to the temptations and tribulations of this earth and about the only thing that could halt their emergence into full consciousness and power was their destruction.

You might ask at this point why those in physical incarnation had only limited roles to play in the support and nurturing of the spiritual emissaries. One reason for this limitation has already been provided. Individuals who operated these schools were subject to the same persecution and temptation as the spiritual emissaries. They themselves had to be protected and the best way to do this was to provide them with only as much information as was necessary for them to fulfill their limited roles.

Another reason for the limited role of these schools had to do with the frailty of the human ego and the weakness of the flesh. Because these schools were a part of this physical world, they could be easily infiltrated and corrupted by elite forces working against the greater good. Once infiltrated, the truths would be corrupted and the schools turned into instruments of bondage. Far better to limit the role of the school and the potential damage that would come from the inevitable infiltration, corruption, and/or destruction of the school than to provide too much responsibility and authority over the critical work of the spiritual emissary.

The interested individual can recognize a corrupted mystery school largely by the form and content of the "truths" they teach. Corrupted schools often emphasize secret knowledge (even while they publicly announce they have such secret knowledge). They often speak about their "God given" tasks and special dispensations, the unworthy masses, or the defiled nature of creation. They can be recognized by the lack of universal love in their teachings, their elaborate and contrived spiritual hierarchies, and the obvious domination of the ego in their work. Members often see themselves as chosen or special in some way. Always keep in mind that the highest spiritual truths are love based and never fear based. They are egalitarian and not hierarchical. They are open to all and not just a selected few.

Corrupted schools are magnets for agents of the dark forces who are assigned the task of tracking down and twisting high spiritual truths. Although you may get the sense that corrupted schools are an unplanned manifestation (i.e., they came about because of a loss of spiritual control), they are not. Corrupted schools are actually encouraged to form (and many spiritual masters actually manifest to create these schools) in order to provide decoys for the ruling elites. The hierarchical structures, organizational layers, and reward structures of these corrupted schools are very attractive to those who sacrifice their higher selves to the domination of the limited ego.

The true teacher will never fail to tell the chela to **go inside** for the truth. External guides can only provide signposts that point the way back inside and up towards Spirit.

Conclusion

In this chapter, we have covered considerable ground. Extending our discussion of the Annunaki in the last chapter we learned how, despite the fact that we have met the preconditions for ascension, we have been kept from it by the machinations of elite groups who have refused to "let the people go." We also learned of the War of Souls that we have had to undertake because of elite refusal to release you from your spiritual bondage. As we saw, the goal of this grand spiritual conflict has been to weaken the hold of the world elites, introduce an Infrastructure of Light, finally awaken the population, and ascend this planet. We began our formal discussion of the War of Souls with the work of the ascended masters. We examined the nature of their activities, the spiritual truths they brought, and their support networks.

In the next chapter, we will continue our examination of the Infrastructure of Light and those who came to build it by discussing individuals and groups who incarnated with scientific, philosophical, or technological contributions that would support the final ascension and awakening efforts during the opening years of the 21st century.

CHAPTER SIX:
EMISSARIES OF LIGHT II

We're off you know,
To a distant land
And the only ones, allowed to come
Are those who feel they can.

Go right along,
With the master plan
Cause the only thing,
You've got to bring
Is sitting there in your head.

Klaatu, from the album Hope

Introduction

As we learned in the last chapter, we have been engaged in a War of Souls against Annunaki minions on this planet for several centuries. This war pitted ruling elites against the energy workers of this earth and the starseeds who came to intervene. In the last chapter, you were introduced to the work of special spiritual emissaries who came to create the spiritual foundation for the Infrastructure of Light. You learned that the primary task of these emissaries was to create an edifice of truth that would be impervious to distortion. Their final strategy had them creating a multi-layered structure of truth and meaning that could be twisted on the surface, but deep within retained the revolutionary truths intact.

In this chapter, we will examine in more detail the work of other incarnated starseeds. These additional workers came to help with the overall strategy by providing higher social, political, and technological interventions. These individuals, and there are many with varied talents and abilities, have been an essential component of the awakening process. There were specialists in technology and education, specialists in raising planetary consciousness, and specialists in social and political reform – to name a few. Without their work, we would never have been able to usurp control over this planet from the elites who have kept us all enslaved. Their contributions, along with the work of the ascended masters, have created, in the final moments of 3D existence, conditions that support a successful awakening and ascension process.

Scientists and Savants

Aside from building the spiritual infrastructure, one of the first steps required to support a general awakening and enlightenment of the world's population was to encourage the enterprise of literacy and education. Although it is true that reading and writing are not prerequisites for profound and deep learning (you can always go directly to the Source or to your guides), it is true that literacy supports learning and makes it more efficient and more resistant to elite control. Keeping a few people, usually priests, literate and in control of the world's learning and everyone else dependent on authoritative pulpit like transmissions of sacred "truths" makes people easy to control. Getting the truth out of the hands of the Brahmin (priest) castes and into the hands of the masses was a necessary first step in building the Infrastructure of Light.

In order to encourage the general edification of the earth's population, many starseeds over many centuries incarnated as teachers and philosophers in order to assist with the general educational effort. They came to introduce, among other things, accessible alphabet systems, egalitarian systems of thinking, and alternative conceptions of the cosmos. From ancient philosophy through to modern science, starseeds in this group are responsible for the gradual growth and spread of education, art, science, and empiricism[16] in all ancient (e.g., Chinese, Arab, European) and modern worlds.

Of course, the ruling classes responded in a predictable fashion to advances in literacy and learning. They were terrified when new systems of thinking and educational innovations where pressed into public service. They quickly saw the potential in an educated and enlightened mass population and feared that such an educated population would

---

[16] Empiricism is a philosophical position that holds that all "truths" should be backed up by evidence. Empiricists hold that we should never claim to know anything unless we can refer to some sort of experiential evidence that supports our claims to truth. Thus, for example, we *know* gravity exists because we can see its effects in the natural world. We also *know* humans are at least potentially aggressive (or loving) for that matter because we can *see* the evidence of this all around us.

The general spread of empiricism was a great advance over the superstition cultivated by the ancient church and state. However, we often take empiricism too far and when we do it can be used, just like we use superstition, to control the population and dismiss knowledge that is threatening to the status quo. This is what happens when scientists, philosophers, or *debunkers* try to dismiss spiritual experience as nothing more than a fantasy or a biological epiphenomenon. The problem here is that they extend the empiricist prescription that we provide evidence for our knowing to mean, "If I don't see it, I don't believe it exists."

This position is seductive to anyone without authentic spiritual experience. However, it is based on an erroneous interpretation of empiricist philosophy. Empiricists have never said that a phenomenon must be visible to be real. If they did, then we would have to dismiss gravity as a real and verifiable phenomenon because not a single individual anywhere has ever *seen* gravity. Obviously, we know gravity exists because of its *effects* on the natural world. In the same way, we know that spiritual experience is valid because we can see its effects on us and those around us. Unless the skeptic is willing to dismiss the experiences of the vast majority of individuals on this planet as nothing more than idiotic ramblings or the product of rank superstition (something any true empiricist would be loathe to do), then the case for Spirit was made several centuries ago.

Of course, direct experience is always the preferred way of assessing the truth of a claim. Those interested in advancing on a spiritual path and having verifiable spiritual experiences are encouraged to step onto The Path with a sincere heart and an open mind.

see through their dirty tricks. Recognizing the threat, they resisted the spread of education and literacy by, for example, wrapping ideas or educational systems inside elite languages and keeping the general population ignorant of these specialized languages (e.g., Latin).

However, starseeds were persistent and over the centuries they gradually whittled away at elite control of education and literacy. Of course, elites resisted at every turn. When, for example, the industrial revolution encouraged a skyrocketing demand for an educated workforce, the ruling elites partitioned the system and provided educational streams to carefully manage levels of attainment and knowledge. Members of elite families went to special schools that were closed (either formally or through an excessively high cost of tuition) to the general population. There they were trained in the ways of power and authority. People in the common streams were confined to lower levels of education and trained with ideological systems (raise your hand please, wait for the bell please, sit quietly and work please) designed to keep them prostrate before authority while giving them enough knowledge to function in emerging industrial and, later, knowledge based economies.

The turning point for education, i.e., the point where it became predominantly an instrument of light, came when elite control of the system virtually disintegrated during and following the 1960s entrance of the flower children. Among their many contributions, these ones opened the doors of higher education in North America (and elsewhere) to many who had been denied this privilege in the past. Their overall strategy has been quite successful. Despite ongoing efforts to make universities and colleges inaccessible (for example by raising fees and restricting resources in desperate attempts to stem demand), enrollments continue to increase.

Of course, just having a university degree does not guarantee you will develop the ability to think critically. You have to be willing to see the truth. Nor is learning confined to educational institutions (as the proliferating self-help literature indicates). The important point here however is not in the specific outcomes but in the general enlightenment encouraged by education and literacy. Over the centuries we have seen a growth in the way people of this earth approach truth and knowledge. Centuries ago, the masses of this planet performed two simple functions; they worked and they ate. Anything outside of that was carefully cordoned off and kept out of their reach by elite propaganda and indoctrination. People were not stupid or without potential. They were simply kept in ignorance and fed lies in order to support and justify their servitude (Divine Right of Kings, Rule by Government, etc.). Bringing the population to a point where they believed they had both the ability to learn and the right to knowledge, and where they approached learning and change as desirable, was a struggle that took our starseeds centuries to accomplish.

Literacy and education were not the only starseed interventions that helped foster a new orientation to truth among the people of this planet. There was also the introduction of science. Nothing supports the elimination of superstition and the quest for truth more than the activities of science. Science has helped bring better dental care, better hygiene, warmer homes, and longer life (among a host of other benefits) and these things make the case for education and learning. Of course, it has not been a completely smooth ride as science coupled with elite prerogative has also been responsible for unspeakable horror. However, despite its negative aspects, science has provided an important contribution to the overall Infrastructure of Light that starseeds came to build.

Of course, if ruling elites resisted any attempts to educate the masses of this planet, they also resisted science and technology. Although this may come as a surprise in an age where science and technology are such pervasive and accepted institutions, the elites actually saw science as a threat. This was especially true in earlier days when the elites used superstition and charlatanry to dazzle, confuse, and justify their privileged positions.

The problem for those in control was that those who came in the name of science generally came with a very powerful challenge. Their challenge was to show that those who held traditional authority as God's representatives on earth (priests, kings, Brahmans, etc.) in fact did not have exclusive pipelines to divine knowledge. When Copernicus came and suggested that the sun was the center of local space, the problem was not so much with the shift in stellar focus but the idea that the priests themselves could be wrong. If they were wrong about something as important as the location of the sun, they could be wrong about many things. Those in authority feared that once people started to question their knowledge and ability, their authority would be quickly undermined. Herein lies the importance of science to our discussion. Its message was simple. Challenge everything. Trust nothing. Always seek the highest truth.

Most of you will be aware of the history of science and know what happened. Even though the elites resisted the spread of truth, and even though they killed and tortured many who challenged their authority, science spread. Interestingly, elites eventually gave in and embraced the very science they originally resisted. They did this not because they gave up their struggle but because they were able to turn science into the handmaiden of elite domination. They realized, for example, that science could replace religion as an ideological system of control. They also found that they could siphon off the wealth that science generated and use it for their own benefit. Finally, they learned that science could create powerful tools of war, oppression, and servitude.

Since shortly after its inception, scientists serving the interests of elite domination have created all sorts of technological terrors with which to kill, maim, and oppress. By the end of the 20th century, science had created ideological systems to justify your oppression (e.g., Social Darwinism), ways to strip the nutrition out of your food (e.g., white bread) and keep your mind dull, and all sorts of biological and chemical straightjackets for your mind and consciousness. The list of infamy that has been perpetrated in the name of science is almost endless.

However, despite the fact that science has come to service elite agendas, in many ways it has remained a tool of freedom. Science, like most human endeavors, is complicated and multi-faceted and in the end, the elites never really had good control of the scientific enterprise. Even in its early days, the expansion of the scientific enterprise outstripped their ability to control and manage the process. The spread of scientific literature, the penetration of the scientific enterprise into the emerging middle classes, and the synergistic effect of the printing press and other technological interventions led the elites into a never ending struggle to contain scientific innovations and twist new truths in ways that supported elite rule. It was a struggle they were destined to lose.

You are a shining example of the successful completion of this struggle. Even twenty years ago, you would have accepted none of what has been said in these pages despite the fact that it is the truth. Your superstition, fear, and paranoia would have prevented you from getting past even the introduction of this book. Even if you had been interested, a book such as this would not make it past elite gatekeepers in the publishing industry. Such a clear and concise presentation would have been halted at the publisher's gate or suppressed shortly after publication. Getting it past the gatekeepers would have required that the truths contained herein be obscured with so much verbiage and esoteric drivel that the book would have been impossible to read.

Things have changed now though, and quite dramatically. This book, and many others like it, can now be published outside of the gate keeping monopoly presses without the need to fool the gatekeepers. Getting the social and political spheres to a point where a book such as this one could emerge, and getting the human populations to the point where they would voluntarily open and read *The Book of Life*, has taken centuries of political, social, and technological intervention.

Communications Technology

If education and science were important components in the elevation of consciousness, communications technology was critical. Not only was such a network necessary for educational purposes (it provided synergistic assistance for other interventions), it was a critical strategic component in the Battle of Armageddon where a sophisticated communications network resistant to elite control would be necessary in order to accomplish the unrestricted communication of truth and the free distribution of spiritual triggers during the final days.

Of course, building the communications infrastructure that we needed was difficult and we constantly struggled against elite attempts to co-opt, dilute, and twist the technological innovations. We tried several times to introduce technologies that would support the type of mass communication that would be a strategic necessity during the end-times struggle. One of our first technological successes came with the introduction of printing in China and later in Europe. Here was a communication medium with considerable potential to enlighten and uplift the population. Unfortunately, while the technology did succeed in spreading literacy and education, it did not attain the revolutionary outcome we had hoped for.

The story is the same as with other starseed interventions. Printing technology was initially resisted by the ruling classes who were threatened by its promise and potential. Their initial resistance turned to glee when they realized that the technology could be used for profit (sale of indulgences, for example), propaganda, and domination. All they had to do, they discovered, was restrict access (i.e., make the press too expensive and complicated for most people to access), keep it close to the corridors of power (buy the newspapers up), and stream it (an elite press for elite ideas and a common press for spreading ideological indoctrination). In this way, the revolutionary potential of printing was weakened as elites took control of the medium.

However, as with other innovations, even though the ruling classes were able to co-opt the technology, printing still contributed synergistically to the overall uplifting of the planet. For example, despite the fact that the printing press eventually became a tool of ideological indoctrination (in every country), it still fostered literacy and it still functioned as a watered down educational tool.

This same general pattern of co-optation and synergistic feedback occurred with related technologies like wireless radio and television. As science advanced and our technological sophistication grew, conditions for the introduction of new technologies were realized. At first, the technologies were resisted by the elites afraid of losing their power. Then they were co-opted and made inaccessible (you see media monopolies in radio, television, satellite, cable, etc.). However, as with science and education, no matter how corrupted the communications technologies became, the general agenda of the starseeds was advanced. Each starseed intervention connected with others and formed an ever-expanding web of education and enlightenment that gradually and inexorably pushed back the darkness on this world.

The culmination of the attempts to build the communications infrastructure or *Web of Light* came recently with the introduction of the World Wide Web (WWW). Until its introduction, no technology has been able to provide a truly democratic, easily accessible, and revolutionary infrastructure that was able to resist all efforts to control and co-opt. With the introduction and explosion of the WWW (from a few advocates in 1989 to a user base of well over ½ billion people), we finally had the powerful technology that, along with all the other starseed interventions, helped tip the "truth scale" on this planet. It is now quite impossible for elites to stem the flow of truth. The total disintegration of elite realities follows swiftly on the heels of this amazing Web of Light.

About the WWW

Those of you who have spent any time working on the WWW will know it is an amazing resource. You can learn about anything on the WWW from Aardvarks to Zoology, and Zen to Ascension by simply learning how to use the web search engines. With powerful search engines collating millions of pages, almost any topic you can think of is available for study. The real kicker is that most information remains free. Putting aside access costs (cost of computer, cost of cable), the WWW has evolved into a place where interested amateurs of any stripe may share their knowledge and wisdom with other interested individuals. The WWW has become our first one hundred percent democratic Information Commons.

It is no accident that the WWW has become such a powerful and democratic information resource. It was designed that way at its technological core. In order to understand this you have to understand how and why the Internet, which is what supports the WWW, was conceived. In 1962, Paul Baran of the RAND Corporation was commissioned by the U.S. Air Force to develop a communication system that would be immune to concerted enemy attack or outright nuclear holocaust. A new communications system was needed because, back then, the only technology capable of managing large armed forces over great distances was the telephone. Unfortunately, the phone network was entirely dependent on monolithic switching stations that controlled all local traffic. If even one of these switching stations was destroyed, it brought down entire swaths of the communication network, profoundly handicapping military communication and capability.

Baran's solution to the problem was a methodology known as *packet switching* where data is broken up into datagrams, marked with reassembly instructions, labeled with the sending and receiving system address, and broadcast out into the network. The individually marked packages find their way to the destination by whatever route is available and are then reassembled in the correct order. The key difference between the phone system and the packet system is simple. Unlike the phone system, which has centralized and authoritative switching stations, the Internet does not. Any computer on the Internet has the full set of software and protocol layers to enable it to be a fully functioning relay station.

This unique and de-centralized control structure made the Internet resistant to attack. The only thing that would bring the Internet down would be a total nuclear holocaust. The structure also made the Internet resistant to attempts to control, limit, or otherwise deny access to information. If you had one computer on a large network of 10,000 computers, and you did not like the information on that one computer, the only way you could stop other computers from accessing that information was to physically shut down the computer. You could not block access from any single point. This of course is not a problem if you only have one offending computer and are prepared to deny the basic right of free communication to your people. However, when everyone starts to take the notion of free speech to heart and starts putting up their own opinions and knowledge, you have a problem. You simply cannot shut down millions of computers broadcasting information out into the Internet. This is especially true when information on the WWW seems to be so disrespectful of the political and sociological boundaries exploited by the elites of this world.

This problem is what faces the elites at the start of the 21st century. How can they possibly stem the rush of information? The problem only gets worse as the cost of computers and access plummets and as each literate person in this world begins to think of themselves as a source of knowledge. With over ½ billion people connected at the turn of the century, and with each of these a potential source of truth, there is no way to prevent the explosion of light that is now illuminating this entire planet. It is truly amazing to behold.

Those of you who make the effort to see through the deceptions of your own national leaders will have seen the power of this network actualized in the second Iraq war. Unlike previous conflicts where information was tightly controlled and funneled through a few selected media channels, in this conflict the war and its horrific images were broadcast globally by multiple official and unofficial news sources. You could get the official USA position by watching CNN, the official Iraqi position by watching Al Jazeera, or the independent Pakistani and UK positions by reading their respective English language web sites. The multiplicity of perspectives is amazing especially when you consider the fact that the WWW did not exist for any previous war. For the first time in history, the biases of official sources, the way government sources like CNN or Al Jazeera spin news to support their own elite agendas, and the outright lies of the elites on both sides of the great ocean were painfully obvious to all who had made the choice to open their eyes to the truth.

It is no understatement to say that the WWW is the crowning jewel of centuries of starseed intervention. It is dependent on and made possible by advances in education, science, and technology over several centuries. Its creation, the massive support given to it by people on this planet, and its incredible potential for giving voice to the average individual signals (like many other recent developments) the end of elite privilege on this world.

Additional Workers

As you can see from even the brief overview of starseed work provided above, several centuries of interventions were required to bring this world to the point where we could initiate ascension and awakening. Actually, it is a bit more complicated than this. As noted at the outset of our discussion on starseed interventions, we have tried several times to trigger ascension and awakening. As each attempt failed, and as we learned more about how to overcome elite resistance, concurrent interventions were ordered in temporal and spatial locations throughout the space/time tube. There were several 'sets' of these interventions – one following each failed ascension and awakening attempt. If you have trouble with this, think back to our discussion of the space/time tube and the distinction between linear time and cyclical spiritual moments.

From the perspective of individuals in body and standing at the edge-of-time, only one set of interventions can be seen. You or I looking back into the tube would see centuries of history unfolding in a strictly linear fashion. The perspective of Immortal Spirit is a bit

141

different. From that perspective we have seen several 'sets' of linear, centuries long interventions. Echoes of these interventions, and the timelines associated with them, can still be *felt* by many spiritually in-tune individuals.

The point here is not to twist your brain but to simply emphasize the amount of work that has been required to get this earth to the point where things were adjusted just right to allow for ascension and awakening. Multiple millennia of linear manifestations have been required. It has been quite the struggle.

However, we have won the day. In our final set of concurrent interventions, we have managed to cook physicality in this area to just the right pressure and temperature to ensure a successful ascension and awakening. As you already know, when we realized that our next attempt to trigger awakening would very likely yield a spectacular result, we initiated the Battle of Armageddon.

With the initiation of the Battle of Armageddon, the final strategic starseed deployments could be undertaken. The final groups of starseeds, who came with the express purpose of fighting in the great battle, began incarnating in the '50s and '60s. These ones were left unconscious until it became clear that the forces of light had won the day. Had the forces of light not been able to achieve their goals, these final waves of starseeds would never have been awakened. They would have gone through the same planetary cleansing that everyone else would have had to endure.

In the rest of this chapter we will look at several of these specialized groups of starseeds. You can consider the revelations about these individuals as another sign of the victory of light. If we could not peer into the future and see the successful denouement of this great conflict, information on these critical volunteers would have never been released.

Healers

One group of starseeds that came with the express purpose of assisting in the Battle of Armageddon were the healers. These individuals are the priestesses, priests, witches, and shamans of this earth. Many of them have deep knowledge of the ways of health, balance, and healing and have come to help lift all those who have experienced psychological, emotional, and spiritual damage at the hands of the oppressive elite system. Given the proliferation of mood altering drugs like Prozac, the skyrocketing rates of depression and anxiety disorders (especially in countries like the USA), and the general spiritual malaise experienced by so many at the start of the 21st century, their talents are sorely needed.

Although these individuals can be found operating in concurrent lifetimes throughout the space/time tube, they primarily came to work during the end-times struggle and the period immediately following the Battle of Armageddon where their talents would be most needed. Earlier concurrent incarnations are primarily for training purposes. Many of these ones are not "of this earth" and as a result, they needed to practice their arts with the resources available on this planet before they could reach full effectiveness. Unfortunately, their earlier work in more superstitious and paranoid times meant they were faced with a high probability of repression, torture, and murder for their heretical ideas.

As these individuals developed and advanced their knowledge of the healing arts, the body's energy systems, and the herbal gifts of the earth, and as they taught that the individual had power over their own health and well being (through nutrition, balance, hygiene, etc.), their activities were resisted. The message they brought that you have power over your own health is a very subversive message. The bottom line is that elites on this planet only rule because you give your personal power to them. You are free to take your power back at any time. Anyone who brings you the message of empowerment quickly finds themselves in conflict with ruling elites. Because of the cruelty of the elites and their determination to keep all of you in bondage, our healers have experienced the vilest repressions (torture, rape, mutilation, etc.) at the hands of the elite police forces.

As a result of their concurrent life experiences, the primary challenge for healers in this lifetime is to overcome the deep fear of persecution that percolates up from their concurrent incarnations. This is no easy task for them. Those who are still struggling should find comfort and direction in the guidance that this current lifetime holds no possibility of them experiencing the same persecutions they have experienced in their concurrent incarnations back in the space/time tube. The great battle has already been won and Spirit is already in control. There is no need to fear the ghostly images of repression that penetrate into the consciousness of this body in this incarnation.

The healers that awaken and are able to step into their power will be critical in the years ahead. Many people have been profoundly damaged by the systems of elite control. The work of the healers will help move them past their dependencies, depressions, and self-mutilating behavior patterns and towards healthier lifestyles where they can, in full consciousness, step onto The Path.

It should be noted that healing does not take a lifetime. The process of moving from disconnection to connection or from emotional damage to psychological health is not a long process. It is easily accomplished within a relatively short period. All that is needed is the correct dosage of truth, responsibility, and personal power.

Warriors

Another group of starseeds that came primarily for the end-times struggle are the warriors. They, like the healers discussed above, entered all parts of the space/time tube on concurrent training missions that would prepare them for the work they agreed to undertake during the Battle of Armageddon. Like the healers, they were persecuted and murdered as they learned to challenge authority, move, and struggle within the confines of elite systems. These souls were strong and powerful entities even before they entered incarnation here. However, the experiences they had while incarnated in physicality on this earth, the sacrifices they made, and the pain they endured has given them, like the healers, a strength and determination of purpose that has made them into a most effective resource. They have agreed to complete one or more of several key ascension and awakening tasks.

One function warriors came to fulfill was as protectors. They came to protect the more sensitive and easily damaged starseeds during the critical early days of the end-times struggle when vibrational balance points had just been transcended and sensitive souls would still experience difficulty incarnating and moving effectively. They came to protect spiritual emissaries, priests and priestesses, and others whose special skills and high levels of empathetic vibration made them chronically sensitive to the low vibration of this earth and the intense pain of souls in this incarnation.

Warriors also came to protect the children who would come to anchor new vibrational levels. These new children (see below), like the other souls who came in bodies that could support higher spiritual vibrations, would be extremely sensitive to the physical and psychological attacks that were endemic to a system designed to disempower and disembowel its own people.

Warriors also came as energetic cleansers. These individuals were given the most powerful tools of energetic stamping available and were sent to stand and help cleanse and re-spin the negative energy that would find final expression during the last days of struggle on earth. This activity would be very important because, as we have seen, one of the tactics the elites use to prevent the ascension and awakening is to encourage negative energetic expression. The warriors who came to this earth had tools that would, once activated, literally wash away swaths of improperly stamped energy and help prevent the elites from halting ascension and awakening as they had in previous spiritual moments.

Finally, warriors also came as purveyors of truth. These individuals are experts at seeing through illusion, at raising consciousness, and bringing liberation to the people. Their tools of liberation are not guns (you cannot liberate with a gun no matter what an elite peon will tell you) but songs and stories that instill seeds of truth and help people vibrate at higher levels.

The primary challenge for warriors in this lifetime, like the healers, is throwing off their fears of persecution and violent death and assuming the mantel of authority and power that comes to them to fulfill their final tasks. This challenge of assuming authority is particularly difficult on this earth where we have always been taught that to assume authority signals arrogance or spiritual immaturity. This is very far from the truth and is more about ideological indoctrination into servitude than an expression of the true desires of Spirit or of God. As Spirit, we are authoritative co-creators with full power and full responsibility for what we create and how we create it.

You can find the entrance of these ones prophesied in the Tibetan Kalachakra Tantra where they are named Shambhala warriors.

Children of a Higher Vibration

We will end our overview of the War of Souls and the Battle of Armageddon with a discussion of children. Children are a critical part of the end-times spiritual struggle on this planet. The reason for this is simple. Children may be brought into manifestation in bodies with fewer limitations than previous generations. As such, children provide the opportunity to lock in spiritual advances on this planet. As certain vibratory base levels are reached on this earth, waves of children who are free of the energetic limitations and karmic entanglements of previous generations are sent to "hold" higher vibrational rates.

The entry of children with progressively reduced energetic limitations is a sign of the spiritual accomplishment of the people of this earth simply because children that come in without energetic limitations can only enter when certain base rates of vibration have been attained. The reason for this has to do with the way our bodies operate and how our chakra systems work. You will recall that in a previous chapter we noted the goal of spiritual development on this planet is to progressively develop and re-open the energy centers in your body (chakras) which, for reasons that can be traced back to Atlantis, are generally closed at birth or intentionally shut off shortly after. The difference between children of higher vibration and those who were born with full energetic limitations before the turn of this century is simply that children with higher vibrations are born with chakras open and functioning at full power at birth.

That you can enter a body with even the base chakra fully open is a significant accomplishment. To understand this you have to recall that chakra centers are expressive centers. When they are weakened, we lack expressive capability (sexuality, power, musicality, etc.). When they are open, we gain considerable expressive power. However, it is sometimes better to have a closed chakra than an open one since an open chakra does not necessarily signal a positive development. If you have an open chakra, the energy MUST be expressed in some fashion. Of course, it is best if the energy finds healthy expression. However, this has not always been possible and in less than ideal political, spiritual, or psychological conditions, the energy is often internalized, directed toward self-destructive ends, or expressed in twisted negativity in the physical world.

Consider the energy of the lower spleen chakra as an example of the expressive possibilities and dangers. The Swadishthan Chakra, which is related to our sexual organs, governs the expression of our desires (both spiritual and material). A blocked (unopened) second chakra means we will be unable to engage in healthy relationships (much less healthy sexual relationships), will garner no physical enjoyment from our existence here, and will make no effort to actualize our desires. We will live a gray, loveless, and lifeless existence (while in body). A healthy second chakra means we express what we want in a healthy and balanced manner. We engage in healthy sexual relationships, have a balanced relationship with food, and pursue our inner desires with maturity and responsibility. A twisted expression of the Swadishthan energy (much more common in the male of the species) will see power, domination, cruelty, irresponsibility, and gluttony enter into our relationships.

An internalized expression of the Swadishthan energy will see our own desires and our own inner needs sacrificed in the martyr like service of others. The archetype here is the wailing mother who sacrifices her entire being for her children and husband. There is of course no spiritual honor in this sacrifice. There is only a slow death preceded by deeper and more intransigent bouts of depression and self-destructive behavior patterns. You can see why it is better to block the energy rather than allow its expression in circumstances where the energy might be internalized. Blocking it until the individual is ready to grow into their power means less suffering and less obstacles to growth down the road.

Obviously, external political, social, and psychological conditions can affect how the energy of a chakra is expressed. In Victorian England with its excessive prudery and restrictive sexual morality, a healthy sexual expression would have been improbable. Expression of the Swadishthan energy would have been cut off or found twisted outlets. However, following the sexual revolution of the '50s and '60s, these energies were largely reactivated and locked into a more positive expression.

At a certain point early in this century, it became possible to send souls into bodies with a fully functioning second chakra. These came to hold the higher vibration. They came into bodies that, because of the activated chakras, would have to find positive expression or risk self-destruction as the energies turned inward. At first, it would have been very difficult for these souls to find proper expression since the external conditions that would support healthy expression were nascent. The ones that came first took a risk for this reason and often failed to find healthy outlets (and self-destructed in one way or another). However, as time passed and more of the front-runners locked in a healthy energetic expression, healthy expression became more prevalent and easier to accomplish. Nowadays, healthy sexual expression is the norm and we may say that the vibration of the Swadishthan chakra has been locked in.

It should be clear from this that another way of looking at the spiritual struggle, other than seeing it as a struggle against elite imposed ignorance, is to see it as a struggle to create the conditions whereby we could progressively allow the opening at birth of the higher chakras. Things like the sexual revolution, the progressive removal of racist idiocies, the gradual removal of religious superstitions, the introduction of truer understandings of the nature of existence, and the gradual maturation of spiritual and intuitive abilities, have all been part of this grand spiritual reconditioning process. As each new plateau was reached, and as each new wave of children with open chakras came, a new milestone in the spiritual development of the people of this planet was locked in.

This is not to say you cannot find the wherewithal to block, twist, or suppress your own (or others') chakra energies. You can still find that (though not for very much longer). Attaining the milestones simply means that, at a collective level, a general reversal of the vibrational conditions becomes almost impossible without truly draconian oppression. At an individual level it means that, all things considered, it is easier for most people to find (if they are honestly looking) the tools and knowledge they need for healthy expression.

Several groups of children with progressively reduced limitations have been sent over the past century to hold new vibrational levels. The most recent groups, Indigo Children and Crystal Children, represent very high levels of spiritual attainment on this planet. Indigo children began arriving on this planet when a few brave souls began incarnating in newly minted milestone bodies during the late 1950s. The mass arrival of Indigos began in the late 1960s and 1970s. By the late '80s, sufficient indigos had entered to lock higher vibrational rates in. At that point, all new children on this planet were indigo.

While it took indigos about thirty-five years to lock in conditions for a healthy expression of the chakra system up to the throat chakra, Crystal Children, who began entering in the early nineties, took fewer than seven. Crystal children (also known in prophecy as the second coming) are completely free of energetic limitations and completely free of karma (i.e., no cleanup contracts). Even twenty years ago these children could not have entered incarnation here because conditions would not have supported the healthy expression of their energetic systems. Either that or the power of their fully functioning systems would have made them targets for those seeking to prevent their occurrence. Now they can be protected and nurtured and can rapidly spread the highest energies onto this planet.

These children are incredibly important. In fact, they are the most important milestones in the history of this planet because they represent the mass return of the fully functioning, fully empowered, fully connected human being. From the tip of their toes to the crown on their heads, they are the new normal. When they began entering in force in 1999, their entrance was yet another sign of the end of the old regimes. Not even Herod could find a way to stop the entrance of millions of Christ children.

Conclusion

In this chapter, we finalized our discussion of the War of Souls and the Battle of Armageddon. Here we learned something of the flavor of starseed work over the centuries. We examined the contribution of the educators, technologists, and savants who came from across the cosmos to help lift this planet out of darkness. Unfortunately, we only scratched the surface of starseed interventions. Much remains to be said about the true spiritual history of this planet. Still, the purpose of the last two chapters was not total historical revelation. They were penned to provide an alternative perspective for those interested in learning the spiritual history of this planet. Others will write a more complete spiritual history of this planet in the years ahead.

In the final chapter of this book, we will take a brief look at your own ascension and awakening process and provide some guidance on how you might facilitate the process. It is important to keep in mind as you read the final chapter of this book that it is necessary for you to move forward. Unless you are one of the ones that have chosen to exit during the grand awakening, and unless you want to experience mass fear and panic as the door to your own awakening, you are advised to get moving now. Nothing can stop the changes that are coming and you can either embrace them or fight them. Those who choose to fight and refuse to heed the calls to awaken and heal will pay higher and higher psychological, emotional, and spiritual costs for their "right" to remain in the ignorance and darkness of 3D.

CHAPTER SEVEN:
YOUR ASCENSION PROCESS

There's a difference between knowing the path,
and walking the path.

Morpheus, from The Matrix

Introduction

In previous chapters of this book we have learned some interesting things about this world as well as some revolutionary "new" ideas about why we are here. Technically, the ideas are not new. Everyone on this planet has known the details of this ascension game from the start. We only forget the details when we incarnate and we only fail to remember through the course of our life because the truth is hidden from us. In the past, there has been a divinely sanctioned reason for hiding the truth. However, now there is no longer any justification for deception and therefore the Truth is rapidly and irrevocably penetrating this reality.

This is very good, and the shift that has allowed this has come none to soon. Our present way of thinking, based as it is on a mixture of Annunaki philosophy and ideological indoctrination, its individualistic, predatorial, consumerist, selfish, ego-centeric, spiteful, competitive, materialistic, and paternalistic orientation has not done us any good at all. In fact, these old ways of thinking have brought us to the brink of political, economic, and ecological disaster. These ways of seeing the world have also brought many of us to the brink of social, psychological, and spiritual collapse. These days only a fool will deny the ecological crises and if you want to know just how messed up we really are, check the rates of mental illness (especially depression) and global use of mood drugs like Prozac for some indication.

There is no point in arguing on the ecological or personal crises we all face. These are facts. If you feel the need to argue with these facts at this point, put this book down now. You are simply not ready for what comes next for you. However, if you are going to continue to read I am going to take it as a given that you accept the need for individual and collective change. I will assume that you have realized you must change yourself first. Finally, I will take it as a given that you have overcome enough of your fear of Spirit (you do not have to be totally fear free to begin this process) that you will be able to trust the process and allow Spirit guides to lead you through the experiences and to the knowledge you will require.

In other words, I will assume you are ready to move forward with your soul's training. I say "your soul's" training here because it is really your soul trying to reach you now. Your soul has been tapping on your shoulder ever since the conditions for ascension and awakening were attained on this earth. The tapping was initially polite and you could ignore it if you wanted to. However, as the new yin energies flood this world and as the point of no return has been passed, the tapping has become increasingly insistent.

The message your soul is trying to get you to listen to is simple.

Listen.

If you are quiet, you can hear it.

Your soul is saying …

"WAKE UP."

"I have some important news for you. The ignorance and darkness you have walked around in for so long is no longer necessary. The poverty, struggle, and violence are no longer needed. The individualist, selfish, competitive, materialistic, spiritually daft approach to life we have all voluntarily endured for so many eons is no longer tolerated."

"You have to WAKE UP."

If the tapping was polite before, your soul is now getting quite anxious to reach you. The reason for its anxiety is simple. Everyone on this planet is out of time. Even now, the conditions on this earth have changed quite dramatically. Children no longer enter this world in amnesia or with Merkaba handicaps. They enter with full power and full remembrance and they enter with the highest vibration. The entrance of these high vibrational crystal children is significant. As more of these children enter and lock in the highest vibration, the vibration of this earth and its biosphere will rocket higher and higher. As the vibration goes up, it will be harder and harder for those who are not moving forward to live within the increasingly energetic environment of this increasingly light filled planet.

As the vibration ascends and the reality of this world shifts, those who are not heeding their soul's call will experience increasing agitation and confusion. The new vibration will quite literally buzz them out of their skin. The longer they wait, the harder it will be to move within the light and the more likely it will become that their soul realizes they will simply not wake up. You want to avoid that soul decision if you can because if the soul concludes that an individual will not wake, it will simply pull the plug. This is bad news for your body, I suppose, but your body is just dust. However, it is Good News for your monad. After it exits your current body, it can be retrained in the spaces between physicality and the spirit world and allowed to re-enter physicality with a new outlook and a fresh new body.

If the soul thinks that there is a chance that you will awake, it will leave you on this earth and keep tapping. However, your soul will not keep tapping forever. It is working against two deadlines. One deadline you already know. This deadline is the point that your soul says "enough is enough" and removes itself from your body. The other point is the collective "enough is enough" point. You really want to avoid this point. Just prior to this point there will be one last globally visible (even to those without a television) wakeup call during which many individuals on this earth will take their own lives in abject Atlantean terror. This last wake up call is the last opportunity to walk through your deepest fears before the vibration from the crystal children gets too high for the un-activated body to live in.

Obviously, since you are still reading these words, you have overcome enough of your fear to want to listen to advice. So given that your eyes and ears are wide open at this point, I will give you some advice on how best to move forward.

Connect with Your Guides

The first thing you need to do if you want to move forward is, if you have not explicitly done so already, connect with your guides. They are the ones that love you and that know you and know your fears and anxieties. You cannot fool these people and you cannot lie to them. They know what your contracts are, where your blockages are, and where your strengths and weaknesses lie. They know you best and they are the ones that will walk you through this process successfully. Some external guru will not do it. Reading these words will not accomplish it. Only by going inside and looking for guidance internally can you guarantee that you will successfully complete the journey in front of you.

How do you get your guides to help you? It is easy. Just give them permission to help. Your guides have been with you since you were born but for the most part they remain inactive. This is because your guides cannot help you without explicit permission. It is simply against the rules of this earth to interfere in your life if you do not want that interference. This is bad news for the banks of this world, but it is Good News for you since it guarantees your personal sovereignty. It is always your choice.

So, choose guidance.

All you have to do is say something like.

"I wish to move forward" or "I wish to advance on The Path" or "Show me the Way" or something like that and your guides will instantly move to start arranging conditions to help you move forward. They will guide your hand picking books, place certain people in your path whose energy you might need, offer you wisdom in synchronistic events, provide gentle guidance through the quiet voice of inspiration (if you are quiet and listen), and otherwise help you move forward.

Just do not give away your power to them. They do not want it.

Keep in mind you have total control over the process. If things are moving too fast and becoming disconcerting, or if you find yourself loosing too much sleep, or if you need time to assimilate new information, just ask your guides to slow the process down. Tell them you need a night or two of rest or some extra time and they will listen, out of love, to whatever you tell them.

The Roller Coaster Ride of Ra

Once you have connected with your guides, any one of several things can happen. What comes up will really depend on your particular circumstances. One of the first things you may be required to do is clear your old karma. If you do have karma to clear, as soon as you give your intent to move forward, the relationships in your life will begin to explode and, eventually, change. This is because many of the key relationships in your life have been what we call karmic setups. In many of your relationships, the only reason you came together at all was to clear karma. Once these setups are no longer necessary, i.e., once your karma is gone, the relationships are no longer necessary.

In order to understand why this is, recall for a moment that one of the reasons you incarnate is to clean up energy. However, just incarnating is not enough. Cleansing energy is a participatory process that involves actively pumping energy through your heart chakra. Your body on its own is not aware of its higher energetic functions and even if it was, it would not normally be willing to draw negative energy into itself. Doing so goes against its basic survival instinct to avoid bad things. Of course, there are times when your body can become dependent on negativity and negative energy. If it is, however, that signals a spiritual pathology that must be dealt with before you can even begin to think of karma. I can only assume that the reader of this text is beyond that.

The point here is that under normal conditions your body avoids negativity. In order that you might encourage your body to draw negative energy into it for transmutation, you form relationships. These relationships, including those with your children, provide the karmic lubrication that fools your body into drawing negative energy for transmutation. In the past, there have been many different types of bad energy so there are many different types of karmic relationships. However, no matter what energy these relationships are designed to trigger, they all have one thing in common that identify them as karmic relationships. They have some type of conflict.

You can identify your karmic relationships with this simple key.

If you got conflict, you got Karma.

There are several steps you need to take to clear your karma. You do not have to follow these in a linear fashion and you can often skip steps. Consult with your guides on this.

One of the first things you should practice is identifying your karmic triggers. To identify your triggers, do the following.

Pay attention to whomever it is that causes you emotional pain of some type. This includes your own children and parents, your neighbors, your animals, etc. These are your karmic relationships. Once you have identified your karmic relationships you can sit down and figure out what it is in the relationships that get you going. Is it an action, a set of beliefs, or a way they behave? Perhaps it is a personality trait (you find them overly aggressive, etc.). The trigger could be many different things so pay attention.

Once you have identified your triggers, write your triggers down. You have now identified your karmic "buttons" (or just buttons for short). These buttons were placed in your body, with your permission of course, by your parents. These buttons are what those around you push when they love you enough to want to be a part of your karmic cleansing. Do not kid yourself here. Love is a factor. Only someone that loves you or who has agreed to some pretty heavy sacrifice will repeatedly bear the brunt of the anger, fear, etc. that they draw through you when they push your buttons. Even if you do your best to hide all that negativity away from them, their higher selves know and are aware of any negative thoughts you think. The emotional energy you pass through you in karmic relationships can be quite powerful and for that reason, monads that are not related to you in some fashion will generally avoid helping you with your karma since it is such a difficult commitment.

Once you have identified your triggers, you need to identify the energy associated with them. You can do that by asking the simple question. What do I feel when my button is pushed? Ask yourself one of the following questions: Do I feel anger? Do I feel superior? Do I feel martyred? Do I feel pain? Do I feel fear? When you have identified whatever it is you feel when this button is pushed, write that feeling down as well. You now have enough information in front of you to identify the energy contracts you came to manage, the way that energy is triggered, and what your opportunities are for dealing with that energy.

Now that you have identified your buttons and the reactions they elicit, it is time to clean up that energy. All you have to do to clear the energy is stop letting it affect you. It is as simple as that. Note that this does not mean ending those relationships that cause you grief. It also does not mean asking or demanding that others stop pushing your buttons out of some misplaced sense of respect or duty. If you do either of these things, you have walked away from your karmic responsibility. You already know your guides will not let you do that so you can expect your next relationship, and your next one, and your next, will all be the same button pushers as you rejected the last time. You will not be any farther ahead by running.

So, if you cannot run and you cannot hide, how do you stop the energy from affecting you? That is simple. Instead of fighting it, giving into it, or pretending it is not there, simply allow it pass through you. Let the emotions wash over you and out of you and let the energy pass through you while you are in a calm and peaceful state. That is "all" there is to it. Of course, while it sounds simple in theory, in practice it is horribly difficult. The first time you try to do this with any particular energy you will likely fail. There may well be years of habitual responses, you may actually like feeling the emotions you feel (e.g., you may like feeling superior, martyred, powerful, etc.), or your body may not want to release the energy because it feeds from it and does not wish to give up its food source.[17] Be diligent in your practice but do not

---

[17] People like this are commonly known as psychic vampires. These are very sick puppies and if they do not smarten up in this world, they

come down on yourself. Every failure makes you stronger and makes your next attempt to transmute the energy more likely to succeed.

There are many things you can do to facilitate this process. If it is anger you feel, try a timeout so that the angry energy has time to pass through your heart chakra. Of course, you have to release the reasons for the anger and let the anger go. Otherwise, you will just exchange anger for anger. If it is fear that binds you in karma, try drawing from the love of Spirit or your Guides. If it is superiority, remember we are all Sparks of The One. If it is pain, explain your pain and ask for solace instead of lashing out in anger. Whatever it is you do, the goal is to allow that energy to pass through your heart chakra in order that it can be transmuted from negative into neutral or positive creative energy.

Fortunately for all of us, it usually does not take long to overcome habitual patterns and clear karma once our eyes are open and we see the karmic relationships for what they really are. Even in the worst cases, (and I mean down in the gutter, hit bottom, nowhere else to go types) it normally takes less than a year to turn things around. They key here is, as the Buddha once said, right understanding. If you think all the bad things that happen in your life are God's way to punish you, or if you think that the natural world is predatorial and out to get you in some way, your self esteem issues will prevent you from moving forward. Despite what Hollywood will tell you, few of us willingly take our chains off if we believe we deserve the chains.

Also, keep in mind your guides. If you are stuck on something or cannot figure a way through a particular karmic problem, ask your

---

transfer their bodily hunger to the monad after death and literally become dark and tiny little energy leaches that hang onto physicality post-mortem. They are the classic "lost souls." All you can do for these ones is shine light on them and calmly and politely tell them to leave your space. There is **no point** and no benefit to them or you in retaining contact. They will overcome their pathology in their own good time or they will return to essence.

guides. They will always answer you in a direct and easy to understand fashion. The answers are sometimes subtle (meaning hard to see or hear) though. So, ask your questions, but pay attention.

Once you have cleared your karma, and you will know that day has come when people are trying to push your buttons and you no longer react to them, the relationships around that had been based on karmic contracts will begin to change. Your button pushers should stop pushing your buttons once their higher selves get the message that you are done and for your part, you should stop looking for situations and button pushers to push your buttons. At this point, the people who had karmic ties may exit your personal sphere altogether and go find some other buttons to push. Or they may, if they are also in a position to clear their own karma, decide to follow you forward. You cannot determine ahead of time what will happen. However, it is far more likely that they will move forward with their own karmic contracts if they **see you** successfully clear yours. If you love them, do not stay behind because you are afraid of losing them. As the vibration of this planet advances you will inevitably manifest exactly what you fear anyway and as a result you will inevitably end up losing them. The only way to avoid this is to just move forward and provide them with the healthy example they need to make the right choice.

If they choose, they will follow.

Be of Service

Most people understand the process of karmic clearing on an individual level. Even in the paragraphs above, I explained the process as primarily an individual process. There is much truth in this. Karmic cleansing is largely an individual process. However, it can also be handled collectively as well. You can lighten significantly your own karmic load (and the load of others) by engaging in collective cleanup work. You can do this by simply helping others and being of service.

Details of how this works to lighten your load are complex and I will not go into them in any detail here. Just consider this. Helping others makes you feel good, makes others feel good (i.e., makes them feel loved, accepted, worthwhile, etc.), and when you are feeling good, you are transmuting energy. It is very much like shining a light in a dark room. Enter a dark room and all the blackness around you is all the negative energy there is. In the room with you are a thousand people all groping around trying to find some way out. When you reach out your hand and help them, it is like lighting a candle in the darkness. Your area is immediately illuminated and those around you immediately see their way forward. They then begin lighting their own candles and helping others. Soon you have an army of people running through a brightly lit room helping others light their candles. It is a very beautiful sight to see.

There is one word of advice and caution here. Being of service does not mean flying to another country and helping foreign nationals or going to the PTA meeting and helping your school if this means leaving your own spouse and children in the dark. Removing your light in this fashion runs a high risk of spreading darkness rather than clearing karma. Start at home, in your neighborhood, and with those in walking distance from you before you take yourself on missions of salvation half way across the world. Leave the missionary work to the missionaries and others with the appropriate calling.

Clearing Blockages

Getting your karma out of the way is about one-half the battle. After your karma is cleared, the next step is to activate your chakra system. Actually, this is not a linear process. You can start activating

163

your chakras while still clearing karma. In fact, activating your chakras is one way to help speed up the events in your life that provide opportunities for karmic cleansing. Keep this in mind if things start moving too fast for you.

There are two steps to the process of chakra activation. The first step is to simply meditate on them. Remember energy follows intent. Find a good diagram of your chakra system so you know where the chakras are located, close your eyes, and draw pictures in your mind's eye of the chakras opening and energy streaming through them. Visualize whatever is intuitive and comfortable for you. You can visualize the chakras as colored energy balls, as flowers opening and closing, or as multidimensional conduits that flush creative energy into this world. See your chakras opening, expanding, and allowing more and more energy through. Do not worry if you have trouble visualizing the energy centers at first. You will get better with practice.

One thing you should be warned about is that when you visualize your chakras, always visualize them operating in balance. Do not give one or another predominance. A balanced energy system is absolutely necessary for the final stages of your activation process so do not ignore this advice. Trust your intuition. If you visualize your system and you sense that one or another chakra is weaker, it is OK to focus more intent on the weak chakras. However, always return to visualizing a balanced system.

Once you have started the visualization process one of three things can happen. The energy might flow normally. Free flow of your chakra energy would be the ideal scenario. Unfortunately, in the ugly world conditions we have endured, this is not altogether likely. One negative possibility is that the energy might start to flow but be turned from a positive to a negative expression. The other negative possibility is that, instead of flowing freely, the energy might **not** flow because there is a blockage. You wish to avoid the latter two eventualities.

Let us deal with blockages first.

Overcoming Blocks

There is only one thing that can block your chakras from passing energy and that one thing is fear. Fear is the exact opposite of Love. Fear is a very powerful tool and can prevent even the most energized systems from passing energy. We cannot go into much detail about fear because it is quite a complicated topic. We will say that there are many sources of fear in our culture. Some of these fears are unintended and come from past trauma. Some fears, the really big ones, come from global events like the destruction of Atlantis. Others come from our current lived experience and can either result from our own experiences or can be imposed on us by the socialization process.

As noted, fear is important because it blocks your chakras from passing energy. There is no deep metaphysical reason for this. The blockage works simply because your fear forces you to reject the energy. Consider your crown chakra. This is your connection to the higher spiritual realms, the consciousness hierarchy, and ultimately God. Your crown chakra allows you to bring higher realities into expression in this world. Unfortunately, most people are terrified of higher realities. They are either scared that the world will end as their connections start to open (as it did when Atlantis was destroyed), or they adopted religious beliefs designed to keep their crown chakra closed. These religious beliefs, like the Christian doctrines that emphasize a spiteful, angry, punitive, and vengeful God, teach you that God will smite you for the many mistakes you made. This fear, like the Atlantean fear of enlightenment, is so powerful that whenever you get an authentic glimpse of the power and glory of Spirit, you cower in

165

terror thinking that you will be damned to eternal fire. Of course, this fear is groundless. Nevertheless, it is there and despite its absurdity, it does prevent you from connecting through your crown chakra because whenever the connection starts, you simply shut it down to prevent having to face your fear.

Another example of the way fear blocks expression can be provided with the second chakra. Your second chakra is associated with creative energies (sex, passion, art, etc.). Fear of your own inadequacy keeps you from enjoying sex or expressing the high creative impulses we all have. You will never learn to paint if you think that only the "talented" can paint. Of course, forty years ago Europeans and North Americans were actually afraid of sex (thought it was bestial, dirty, primitive, etc.). That was a horrible fear that kept the second chakra almost totally shut. Thankfully, the spiritual master Elvis Presley (The King) was able to (along with others who came for this purpose) overcome that particular fear on a global scale. Of course, like all masters, his high vibration meant it was very difficult and painful for him to live in the world as it existed at the time and he eventually succumbed to the mind and body numbing powers of alcohol and narcotics to dull what must have been an increasingly difficult and painful existence.

There is only one way to unblock a chakra blocked by fear. You have to walk through that fear. You have to face your demons. This is not something you can do intellectually. It is a highly emotional, visceral experience. Your body actually has to experience the fear and walk through that. No amount of intellectualizing or emotional tricks will suffice.

The reason you actually have to experience your fear and walk through it has to do with the way fears are stored in your body. Even today, fear has survival value. Fear tells us to avoid high places, avoid angry mobs, and avoid rabid dogs. However, fear only has survival value if it can be transferred from the body that experiences it to other bodies. Thankfully, this is possible. Emotions that you experience, and the events associated with them, are imprinted on your DNA structure. This DNA structure, which as earth scientists are beginning to realize is far more complex than originally thought, exists in multiple dimensions, records everything, and makes the emotional associations you generate available to other individuals in genetic "proximity" to you.

The imprint of your fear and its location in your DNA can be thought of as a computer program stored on your computer's hard disk. The only way to change the program (imprint) is to write over it. The only way to write over it is to find the program's location on the disk and move to the first bit of the program. When the computer has located the program, it can then write a new program (or random sets of bits) over it. However, in order to get to the first bit of the program (imprint) you need an address. On your computer, the address is a binary number that locates the physical spot on the disk where the program is located. In your genetic structure, the address is an event association. In order to overwrite the original program or imprint, you have to use the right address or event association.

For example, overwriting the deep fears that were imprinted in our genetic structure by Atlantis means experiencing the same event. Only by experiencing the same event (or an event similar) is our DNA, which has a storage capability far beyond the wildest imagination of computer theorists, able to access the location of the original imprint. Once you invoke the event (word to the wise, the event can be invoked either internally or externally) and your body/mind has accessed the appropriate location in DNA, you have an opportunity to change the programming.

I say opportunity because it is just that, an opportunity. There is no guarantee that we overcome our fears and we may turn and flee rather than confront our terror. Sadly, our societies, based as they are on Annunaki control strategies, do not give us the tools we need to overcome our fears. In fact, our ruling classes actually go out of their way to undermine our ability to deal with our fear. For reasons that should be obvious now, they want to ensure we never re-imprint our fears and never open our chakras. They do this by undermining our self esteem, adding to our fears, confusing the DNA locating mechanisms with all sorts of experiential garbage, locking us out of our own chakra systems, and teaching us (above all) to lie to ourselves that we are not afraid.

Now you now why you have to walk through your fears in order to clear them. You must invoke your fear in order to find the right event association (DNA address) so that you can reprogram your DNA computer. There is no way around this.

It is important to consider the fact that it can be quite difficult to provide opportunities for you to walk through your fear. This is especially true with global fears like the Atlantean fear of destruction or the Annunaki bred fear of God. Currently, it is still possible to manifest experiences that provide these opportunities. However, as more people face their fears and move into the Love of Spirit, the opportunities will eventually disappear. At that point, it would be unlikely your higher self would wish to remain on this earth in a handicapped manifestation device without opportunities for healing.

There is not much more I can say here since this is something you do on your own. However, when it comes down to facing your fears you need to remember to trust Spirit. You can help program your body to remember this by reciting the words "I trust Spirit" every morning and every night for a month or two. Then, when the time comes for you to face your biggest fears, you will remember that Love RULES this universe.

The table below provides some hints on what fears are associated with what chakras and what the etiology of specific fears are. This guide might be useful to you as a meditation tool.

Table Two: Chakras and Their Associated Fears[18]

Chakra	Associated fears	Etiology
Crown	Fear of God. Fear of Enlightenment. Fear of the Spirit world. Fear of your higher self.	Destruction of Atlantis. Religious systems that teach you about a mad god or demons and devils bent on destroying you.
Third Eye	Fear of the Truth. Fear of facing your own weaknesses (truth about yourself).	Mostly from current school system and/or belief systems that denounce spirituality. School systems provide years of tests that rank you and tell you just how inadequate you are. They are despicable systems really.
Throat	Fear of your own voice. Fear of speaking your mind.	Mostly from the current school system that undermines your self-esteem, silences you (do not talk in class), and makes you grovel before authority.
Heart	Fear of Love.	Mostly a male fear. Placed by parents who teach boys to be separate (includes such ideas as men do not have emotions, cannot connect, are not nurturing, etc.) Can also be placed in women through the experiences of incest and rape.
Solar Plexus	Fear of Power	Destruction of Atlantis. Also a female/lower class/working class/lower middle class fear. Placed by parents who teach silence and submission through morality plays that emphasize that destruction follows those who take power.
Sacral	Fear of creation. Fear of sex. Fear of having "accidents."	Antiquated teachings of sex. Sense of creative inadequacy. Hollywood star system and lies about "talented."
Root	Fear of Mother Earth. Fear of grounding. Fear of connection.	Comes from systems that teach nature is "red in tooth and claw," predatorial, instinct based, and savage. Also from religious systems that teach God punishes, expects confessions, etc.

---

[18] For a more detailed look at chakras and how to unblock and heal, see my *Dossier of the Ascension: A Practical Guide to Chakra Activation and Kundalini Awakening.*

Right Expression

Hopefully you have already walked through your biggest fears and are now only working on cleaning up the last of the fear imprints. After you are free of your fear, the next big spiritual task is to find positive expression for the energy that will flow through your chakras. As soon as you start to visualize energy flowing out from your chakras, this energy will become available to you. You need to pay attention to how this begins to manifest in your body and your life because your chakra energy will not always lock onto positive expression. In fact, in our societies, finding a positive expression can be very difficult simply because there are many temptations that draw our chakra energy into less optimal expressions.

Despite what the church might have told you about temptation being sent by God to temper the soul, temptation is simply an Annunaki control strategy. One of the things the Annunaki have done to prevent us from accessing our power, besides closing the chakras with fear, was to work to attach chakra energy to negative expressions. By doing this they could ensure that, when some of us did manage to get the chakras spinning, the energy would not manifest towards freedom and light but would instead be expressed in a fashion that helped to maintain the power of the Annunaki.

Some of you reading this and who like to do things like party hard, drink, engage in wanton acts of sexuality, gamble, engage in aggressive and violent sports, or otherwise express your power and creative energies in less than salutatory ways may resist these words. You have been taught that anything goes and that all expressions are permissible as long as you do not hurt anyone else. After all, you only have one life to live and you have a right to enjoy it.

Right?

Wrong!

If you believe that, you have two choices. Continue believing that and put this book down or put that silly individualistic and terribly spiritually misinformed belief aside. Everyone who knows The Path will tell you that The Path is narrow and difficult to walk (at least at first) and requires considerable moral and spiritual rectitude. This is just another way of telling you that you must find right expression for your chakra energies.

Now of course you are still free to do whatever you want so long as you do not hurt anybody if that is what you choose (remember, energy does not care how it is expressed). However, there is a final step in your spiritual activation that you cannot complete until you have found right expression for all your chakra energies. This step is known as Kundalini activation. Kundalini activation is what the world elites have worked so hard to prevent by implanting fear, strewing temptation in front of you, and otherwise murdering those who had achieved it. Kundalini activation is what the world elites are so terrified of. Even one person with activated Kundalini is a significant problem. Thousands are an unstoppable force.

We will examine Kundalini activation in the next section. Before we get there, however, I offer you table three. It contains some examples of right and wrong expression of chakra energy. As with table two, you may find this outline a useful meditation device.

Table Three: Expression of Energy

Chakra	Right Expression	Wrong Expression
Crown	Communication with hierarchy of consciousness. Communication with higher self.	Unlike the lower chakras, this one cannot be expressed improperly. It is either open and feeding your divinity into this world (in which case there is a powerful influence on the expression of all others) or it is closed by fear.
Third Eye	Right Sight. Access to spiritual power. Access to concurrent lives. Access to guides. Allows you to see higher realms.	Ego involvement in spirituality. Ego not as "I" AM GOD but as I am a body. Using your advanced psychic senses for power and domination.
Throat	Right Communication. Respectful, truthful, honest, love based communication. .	Abusive communication. Communication to oppress or hurt. Communication to express domination over another or superiority of ego.
Heart	Right Love. Love used to nurture. Love used to help an individual grow and find **right expression**.	Love used to suffocate, control, and possess. Love in service of ego (love as personal sacrifice).
Solar Plexus	Right Will. Power used to create and express divine will into this reality.	Power used to dominate, steal, or exert your will over others. Power without empathy or sense of greater connections. Power used in service of ego.
Sacral	Right Creation. Healthy sexual relationships. Positive creativity.	Creation through destruction. Power, violence, and domination in the creative acts (including sex). Immature sexuality (playboy ethic).
Root	Grounded. Present in this world. Care for Mother Earth	Flighty, disconnected, ethereal, lost in the clouds. Destruction of Mother Earth. Overly materialistic.

As you might guess, much of our wrong expression of chakra energy is based on wrong ideas about what is right and moral. The Annunaki and their minions have put much nonsense into our heads in order to encourage our energy to flow in the wrong directions. I can offer some general advice on right thinking here but use your own discernment to discover all the keys.

If you are sexist, i.e., if you believe in any way that the male form is superior to the female, you have to change your ideas. Spirit is not gendered. Spirit just is. We are all One in Spirit. Remember, male and female are only forms of energy (yang/yin) and you need both to create and both to get your chakra system working. Both yin and yang need to be in balance and both must have equal power or creation will be difficult. One is not better than the other is. If someone ever tells you that one gender is superior, he or she has a seriously misplaced idea of Spirit. Male and female are just expressions of creative energy and nothing more.

Any notions of hierarchy and entitlement based on hierarchy will have to go as well. There is no hierarchy in Spirit. We are all equal. We are all Sparks of The One. We are all important. We all have the same potential. None of us deserves to be better fed. Nothing you want is denied as Spirit. Nothing you desire is impossible for any body. If we have different talents and abilities on this earth, it is because we have chosen these, not because we have been endowed with them by God. We all deserve peace, prosperity, true wealth (this does not mean the latest and biggest SUV), and happiness. Notions of hierarchy and entitlement tend to get in the way of several of your chakra energies.

Concepts of authority have to go as well. Authority is a worldly thing. You are a spiritual co-creator. You work with God and answer only to God (who is also yourself) on how to manifest love and light on this earth. Belief in the superiority of rulers is a reflection of your own fear, based in your own lack of self-esteem. Once your higher chakras are activated, you are your own best source of truth. You are the captain of your soul.

These conceptual revisions are just a start. As you communicate with your guides, keep your mind open to ongoing revisions in your thinking. We are filled with so much disinformation on this planet that it often takes several iterations before we get reasonably close to the truth.

The Ultimate Goal

The process of clearing your karma, unblocking your chakras, and finding positive expression of your energy can take a bit of time. Be diligent and keep your guides in mind throughout the process. Be patient as well. The process does not take as long as it used to and there are more supports appearing for the process every day. Be honest with yourself. You will progress faster if you admit your weaknesses and overcome them.

Once your karma is cleared and your chakras activated the real fun begins. At the point when all your chakras are bright and spinning, and they have all been aligned properly, it becomes possible to complete your connection to the universal creative pool. Once you are connected, it becomes possible to draw massive amounts of creative energy into this physical dimension. Really, there is nothing in your mundane materialistic 3D world that prepares you for this glorious experience.

Well, that is not quite true. You only have to look to the life of Christ or other ascended masters to know what is possible here.

Completing your connection is very much like completing an electrical circuit. It involves taking a cosmic wire that sits at the base of your spine (called the Kundalini) and running that wire through each aligned chakra, pushing the wire through your crown chakra, and grounding the energy that flows down into you into the earth below you. When connected in this fashion, you can think of your body as one giant electrical circuit with your chakras acting as cosmic light bulbs. When everything is in working order, the juice flows and you light up like a roman candle.

This process has been variously described as the awakening of the Kundalini, the opening of the seven seals, or the descent of the Holy Spirit. It is an event of major personal and collective significance because each individual that completes this process becomes a very powerful conduit for divine intent on this planet.

Graphically, the Kundalini connection process is represented by the medical symbol the caduceus.

Figure Eight: Caduceus

In the above image of the Caduceus, we see the Kundalini wire represented by the twin serpents. In the image, the Kundalini moves from the root chakra through the third eye connecting each to the other in a circuit that is completed as the wire finally connects and passes through the crown into the higher dimensional realms. It is no coincidence that healers have chosen the image of a fully functioning chakra system and activated Kundalini to represent the ultimate goal of their disciplines.

As noted in the section on right expression of energy, until you are ready, your Kundalini will not be activated. When you are ready, you will have no more use for writings like this. Little else needs to be said on this topic.

Nutrition and the Body

I have one final set of comments before I close this chapter and end this book. As you give your intent to move forward, as your karma is cleared, your chakras activated, and you are eventually given a full connection, you need to pay attention to your body's need for sustenance. Listen to what the healers have been saying for centuries. Cleanliness, nutrition, and balance in all things are the keys to a healthy body and healthy mind. There is a reason why our food supply has been poisoned with processed food, stripped of its nutritional value, filled with chemicals, and put in convenient little boxes. When we lack appropriate nutrients, our ability to function is impaired.

As you move forward with this process, you want to provide your body with as much nutrition as you can. Avoid processed foods like the plague they are. They offer little or no nutritional balance and several hundred types of chemicals that come together in dangerous and unpredictable ways in your body. Reduce (you do not have to eliminate) your dependence on meat as well. There are several reasons you should do this, including the possibility that our food supply will collapse and generate significant disease as it did for us in Atlantis. Even if that does not happen, though, spiritually it is unwise. Killing animals generates karma in the best of circumstances (there is a reason why indigenous people were so apologetic and thankful when they killed an animal for food). However, the filthy killing floors where our meat comes from today generate much negativity (cows have heart chakras too, you know). You are responsible for the negativity if you partake in that particular food chain. In any case, with the proliferation of vegetarian cuisines, there is no longer any reason to make dead animals the center of every meal.

It is not expensive to eat healthily if you eliminate processed foods, reduce your meat intake, and spend some time looking for what stores sell what foods cheap in your area. You may find you reduce your food bill by fifty percent or more.

You will also need to drink more water especially during certain phases of the activation process. You may also want to try eating more citrus fruit or squeezing a hunk of lemon into your water for the extra vitamin C you will need. As always, pay attention to things. If you body is thirsty, give it water. You do not want it to burn out in the final activation stages.

Remember, everything in balance.

Conclusion

In this chapter, we applied everything we have learned about the nature of this world to your own individual ascension process. As you can see, understanding your own ascension is not that difficult. It is simply about awakening your chakra system and connecting that system up in kundalini activation.

Of course, while this is conceptually or intellectually easy to understand, the actual process can be quite painful and dramatic. You have to walk through some deep fears and walk a path of the strictest moral rectitude (of course you do get to enjoy sex and have fun as long as you do it in right fashion). Finally, when you are ready, you get to light a fire under your bottom unlike any fire you have ever seen or experienced.

But do not just stand there.

Get moving!

You probably have a lot of work left to do. Start your activation process, raise your fears, clear your blockages, and find right expression of your energies. As we will see in the conclusion to this tome, if you do not activate your chakras and heal your fears voluntarily over the next eighteen months or so, it will be done for you by the chain reaction of manifestation that is being set in motion by the global activation of the higher chakras. The external manifestation of our world's deepest and darkest fears, and the gruesome potential of that expression, is not something that can be prevented. The only way to stop what is coming (or reduce the impact) is to get as many people to willingly walk through their fears as possible so that the collective manifestation of buried fears by those who remain "behind" will be less dramatic. Nothing else, no amount of intellectualizing, waffling, or whining, will stop what is coming.

CONCLUSION

I know you're out there. I can feel you now. I know
that you're afraid... afraid of us. You're afraid of
change. I don't know the future. I didn't come here to
tell you how this is going to end. I came here to tell
how it's going to begin. I'm going to hang up this
phone and then show these people what you don't
want them to see. I'm going to show them a world
without you. A world without rules or controls,
borders or boundaries. A world where anything is
possible. Where we go from there is a choice I leave to
you.

Neo, from The Matrix

If you have made it all the way through this book to the
conclusion, some congratulations are in order. Chances are you are now
sporting a shiny new outlook on the world. The way you think about
things like karma, past lives, time, your own life, and The Ascension
has been fundamentally and permanently altered. If you pause for a
moment and consider your own journey from there to here, you can
see that any one person has a lot to do if they want to successfully walk
The Path. Many things can turn you from this path including
misconception, deception, fear, and temptation. There are even those
who consciously and vigorously pursue your spiritual destruction and
physical and mental enslavement. It is certainly accurate, as some have
said, to say that The Path is narrow and filled with pitfalls.

Thankfully, however, The Path is getting easier to walk. There has
been so much light let in by starseed intervention, so much work done
by the original souls who incarnated on this planet, and so many
individual awakenings that The Path grows wider every day. Truth of all

varieties is becoming more "in your face" and is becoming increasingly difficult to ignore. As time passes and as more people accept the truth and let light shine through them, following The Path will become easier and stepping off it or ignoring that it even exists will become more and more difficult. As more people successfully walk The Path, a day will soon come when the old world of duality will simply flicker out of existence. That day, the "shift day" as we might call it, is going to be a bit of a shocker for those who refused to move. There may be disorientation and confusion but do not worry, you'll be there to help them out! When somebody reaches out a hand for assistance, be sure to pull them into the lifeboat!

If truth be told, the change to the new world is happening even now and as more and more people choose life and face truth, you will see an accelerating change in global consciousness. The masses will no longer tolerate war, poverty, disease, and inequality. There will be no need for them. The new knowledge and wisdom that will blossom forth from science and spirituality will ensure that we are no longer subject to deception, theft, and destruction at the hands of a callous group of world elites. It will be a glorious intellectual enlightenment as we have never seen on this earth and it will be truly amazing to watch. Of course, intellectual enlightenment is not the only enlightenment to look forward to. We can also expect emotional and psychological health as well. In fact, we can all have these things today if we so choose. There has been so much work done that anyone who is interested in finding out how to be emotionally and psychologically healthy will find that the "truth is out there." Truly, there are no more excuses for ignorance.

However, even these enlightenments, as grand as they will be, only represent a fraction of the shift that is going to occur on this planet. In order to get a sense of the magnitude of this shift, recall from our discussion in the first chapter that our purpose on this planet was to generate enough momentum and excitation to push this physical universe back up the Tree of Life. As you will recall, we did this by unbalancing the energy of creation. We introduced more and more yang. As you now know, the introduction of unbalanced creative energy did the job for us, but it messed up a few things up along the way.

Now, however, something divine this way comes. With ascension accomplished, we do not need to work with out of balance energy any more.

Now we can have our yin energy back and indeed now we do.

At the end of 2002, Immortal Spirit put a new electromagnetic grid in place around this planet. The old grid painted all energy coming in with the quality of the masculine yang. The new grid balances the energy. When the new grid went online and the energy started to flow, it was a major milestone in the spiritual history of this planet. You can see just how far you have come in your understanding because you can now understand the full implications of this new grid. You will understand that the completion of the grid signals the end of the old, competitive, patriarchal, and yang based world and its balancing with a more spiritually in-tune and sensitive yin based energy. And, what's even better, no matter how much people scramble to maintain these old world structures, it will be impossible to sustain them in the new balanced energy. There will be simply no energy for them and they will quickly crumble away like the relics of old consciousness that they are.

There is much that could be said about how the old world will crumble (and is even now crumbling) and how we can help everyone accept the new balanced energy. This we can discuss in subsequent books. By way of concluding this book and in order to show you just how far your understanding has advanced, I would like to explain something of what will happen on this earth in the coming short years.

First, I would like remind you of our previous discussion of the chakra system. Recall how we said the top three chakras are powered primarily by yin and the bottom three primarily by yang. Because of the previous imbalance of yang and the lack of yin, the higher chakras (spiritual connection, spiritual truth, spiritual communication) were choked for energy. They did not have the necessary fuel they needed to function; as a result, they atrophied and became activated only under the most grueling spiritual conditions.

Now consider the yin energy flooding into this earth.

Realize there is now fuel for the top three chakras.

Think what is coming.

It is a very divine event!

Between 2003 and 2005, everyone on this earth will be going through higher chakra activation and I do mean everyone. Even now, the higher chakras of many individuals are spinning faster and sparking livelier than they have in millennia. By the end of 2005, not a single person on this earth will be able to avoid this process. It is, after all, a simple physical event. When you pump a room full of oxygen and light a match, you get a big fire. Similarly, when you fill the earth with yin, the once dormant chakras suddenly have the fuel they need and they immediately start to spin regardless of intent. Apply intent to that, and trigger a spiritual awakening, and you get an explosion. With the new energy flooding into this earth, and the way spiritual masters are throwing around spiritual triggers like they were candy, there is no way, short of the death of the physical body, to stop this activation in your own life.

Exciting, is it not?

It is really quite difficult to capture in words what this will mean for people since all of you are going to have different experiences. However, for the sake of illustration we can split this up into two

183

general groups of people. On the one hand, we have those who want to do it the easy way. On the other hand, we have those who want to do it the hard way.

Let us deal with those who want to do it the easy way first.

Those who want to do it the easy way will enjoy the coming months and years and will gaze in wonder and love at the changes unfolding around them. They will find it relatively easy to navigate The Path. They will trust the process, trust God, trust themselves, and trust that others around will follow as well. They will not be too concerned with the darkness that envelops their sisters and brothers (although they will make an example for Spirit by helping those in need) because they know that those who will not awaken right now have exercised their right to choose and in any case, there is nothing wrong with staying back a little longer. It just delays the inevitable awakening. Eventually, everybody will open their eyes. They will have to. It is inevitable. As this process progresses and more and more spiritual light enters this planet, it will eventually be impossible to stay sleeping. Barring accident, the malicious actions of others, or self harm, the bright light of Spirit and God will wake everybody up no matter how deep the sleep.

Those who are going forward the easy way will shortly remember we are all divine Sparks of The One and are all part of a grand tree of consciousness. As their chakras activate, they will rapidly see their deepest desires for peace, harmony, love and balance manifest in the world around them. They will see others struggling with the new energies and they will reach out to help them navigate and move forward. Despite the tribulations of those around them (which will diminish over time as more and more people awaken and move forward) these individuals will welcome the changes.

Those who have chosen to do this the hard way are another matter. They will not trust the process. They will not allow Spirit to guide them. They will dig their heels in, claw back their old beliefs, believe God is punishing them, and will come to see everyone around them as enemies. They will gaze at this world and instead of seeing the emergence of heaven on earth, they will see only the collapse of their old power and authority structures and it will terrify them. As the changes progress and the new utopia unfolds, they will become increasingly unbalanced. As their higher chakras spin faster and brighter, the spiritual voices in their head will grow louder and louder. Being locked in the materialism of 3D existence, they will not understand the voices of their higher self and they will attempt to flee. Insanity may overtake them and they will, ironically, become the very demons they have been taught to fear. They will scream, gnash their teeth, claw at those around them, and lash out in hatred. When finally the day comes for them to walk through the terrible fear of God that was implanted in them at the destruction of Atlantis, their bodies will either join us on the other side of their fear, or they will leave this earth by their own hand. Despite their best efforts to maintain the old world, in the end, they will be unable to halt the changes.

One last note before we close. Many people out there are already beginning to relive the last days of Atlantis. The reason for this is simple. As the new balanced energy pours into this earth, even those with terribly blocked chakras are finding enough energy to manifest the deepest and darkest fears of their higher chakras. As you will recall, this was the original problem in Atlantis. When the time came to reconnect (balance energy), things blew up in our faces.

Just as in Atlantis, as the new yin continues to flood this earth there will be nothing we can do to prevent our sleeping sisters and brothers from manifesting their deepest fears. Even their guides will be unable to help. As the new energies continue to flow, and as our poor sisters and brothers feed off their own terror, it will be an explosive display.

For your part, it will be important to remember that this is not Atlantis. One of the primary reasons for all the starseed interventions on this earth (aside from dealing with the Annunaki pawns) was to ensure that when the time came to rebalance the energy and awaken the population, there would be enough bodies already awake and empowered to prevent the sleepers from manifesting widespread death and mayhem as they did in Atlantis. We have achieved this. Remember in the coming years that enough of us are awake to prevent another Atlantis.

So, when you gaze up at the terrible events that will occur as our sisters and brothers externalize their fear, and when you see all the terrified people screaming in horror and disbelief at what they have unwittingly manifested, shine your light on them and help them face their fears. Walk them through their "days of darkness" and show them the door to the new world by explaining to them that all they have to do to be free of their fear is realize they are creating it, walk through it, and join us on the other side. Once they have realized they are creating their world they will easily walk through their fear and join us on the other side where we all finally remember that we are now **and always have been** master architects of the Divine World Order.

ABOUT MICHAEL SHARP

And long ago and far away,
A prophesy told of this day.
When no more death on Earth there'd be
And balanced true to nature be.
And children laugh and dance and sing,
As joyous would society bring,
A new days dawn, for us to bring,
A warriors song for all to sing.

From the poem *Shambhala Warriors*
By Michael Sharp

Ever since he was a young child, Michael Sharp has been interested in spiritual things. However, up until a few years ago, his interest was largely peripheral to his more worldly concerns. He was born catholic, received a traditional education in the catholic school system, and went on to earn a traditional PhD from a large Canadian university where he has focused on traditional academic things. He eventually completed his academic training with undergraduate degrees in both psychology and sociology and a PhD in sociology. His study and work as a sociologist made him aware of the form and nature of injustice, poverty, and inequality in this world. As a sociologist, he has understood the limitations of world political systems and the way these systems are set up to privilege a few while exploiting the many. However, none of his traditional training, either in the catholic or scientific churches, prepared him for the spiritual awakening that was initiated by the now infamous 9/11 terrorist attacks in the USA which he witnessed while on vacation with his family in Disney World, Florida.

To make a long story short, Michael Sharp went from curious agnostic and primarily materialist to mystic in a little less than four years. While the awakening was gradual for the first two years, the process kicked into high gear for him after he resolved some of his deeper past life fears. One day, he simply sat down at the computer and the ideas began to flow.

Some of the ideas where familiar to him in this incarnation but some were totally outrageous when compared against traditional (scientific or church) canon. The first thing that issued forth from his pen was a completely revised story of creation that revealed truths about this universe and our role in it that had long been suppressed. This poem, entitled The Song of Creation, is available on his web site at the URL http://www.michaelsharp.org/genesis/

The Song of Creation was followed, in rapid succession, by a series of Ascension Poems that pointed to and highlighted various features of our current situation on earth. In *The Shambhala Warriors*, for example, Sharp draws out some of the implications of the prophecies in the Tibetan Kalachakra Tantra where it is foretold that during the end-times a group of specially trained warriors would come to this earth to clear away the darkness and allow the people to move towards spiritual light and freedom. In the poem *The Redemption*, Sharp issues a clear and precise call to all those who are working to preserve the old energy systems on this earth. In his poems *The Wizard* and *Judgment*, Sharp finds a perfect cadence for the energies of the Warrior. Michael Sharp's Ascension Poems are available at his website http://www.michaelsharp.org/

After writing his early poems Sharp went on to extend the information provided in *The Song of Creation*. Filling in the details, a book began to emerge. In this book, which you have in your hand,

Sharp presents a clear, and virtually undistorted revelation of the basic spiritual truths of this planet. As one commentator notes,

> The picture of Reality that [he] presented was so breathtakingly grand, so unbelievably comprehensive and spiritually beautiful, I said to myself that I would rather try this configuration of the truth and be wrong, than be right about anything else that I had ever come across….I felt I had stumbled in from the cold and dark, welcomed into a friend's house that had everything that I needed for sustenance, freely given with love. I found that all the Truth that I had ever learned on my journey started to fit together. I was finding answers to the unanswered questions that had been draining my life of purpose and joy. I was finally able to put my puzzle pieces together, and the picture of Truth that has emerged for me is one of stunning beauty.
>
> Now, my physical health is getting better and I am on my way to gaining control back over all aspects of my life.

> Kelley Gardener

Sharp continues his writing in subsequent works. His second book is entitled *The Dossier of the Ascension* and his third is entitled *The Book of Light*. If *The Book of Life* placed the reader on the Lightning Path of enlightenment, the *Dossier of the Ascension* takes the reader on the Lightning Path of spiritual empowerment. Taken together, *The Dossier of the Ascension, The Book of Life, The Song of Creation,* and *The Book of Light* are extremely powerful catalysts for personal awakening and spiritual empowerment.

INDEX

ABUNDANCE, 68, 70, 100

ACTIVATION, 80, 81, 99, 115, 125, 163, 171, 177, 178, 182

AMNESIA, 89, 90, 92, 94, 95, 97, 123, 125, 154

ANNUNAKI, X, 104, 109, 110, 111, 113, 115, 127, 128, 152, 166, 167, 170, 172, 184

ASCENDED MASTER, 123, 124

ASCENDED MASTER SUPPORT NETWORK, 124

ASCENDED MASTERS, 118

ASCENSION BOUNDARY POINTS, 31

ATLANTEAN EXPERIMENT, 83

ATLANTIS, 58, 62, 80, 81, 83, 85, 86, 90, 91, 94, 99, 101, 104, 105, 110, 113, 115, 146, 164, 166, 169, 176, 184

AWAKENING, 37, 42, 56, 59, 60, 109, 110, 111, 114, 115, 116, 117, 118, 120, 121, 122, 123, 124, 127, 129, 140, 141, 144, 145, 150, 153, 174, 177, 182

BALANCE, 29, 33, 34, 35, 47, 62, 63, 65, 66, 67, 70, 71, 78, 79, 80, 81, 83, 85, 87, 89, 91, 95, 99, 100, 103, 142, 144, 163, 173, 176, 177, 181, 183, 184

BATTLE OF ARMAGEDDON, 117, 118, 135, 141, 142, 144, 145, 150

BLOCKED CHAKRAS, 77

BRAHMANS, 133

BRAHMIN, 129

CADUCEAS, 175

CATHAR MONK, 55

CAVE OF CREATION, 57

CHAKRA, 73, 74, 77, 78, 81, 83, 101, 104, 105, 107, 108, 125, 146, 147, 148, 149, 157, 160, 162, 163, 164, 165, 167, 170, 171, 172, 173, 174, 176, 177, 181, 182

CHAKRA ADMINISTRATORS, 100

CHAKRAS, 73, 74, 77, 78, 79, 80, 81, 82, 85, 88, 89, 90, 94, 99, 101, 124, 146, 148, 162, 163, 164, 167, 168, 170, 172, 173, 174, 176, 177, 178, 181, 182, 183, 184

CHRISTIAN, 164

CNN, 139

COMMUNICATIONS TECHNOLOGY, 135

CONCURRENT LIVES, 52, 54, 172

CONTROL FREAK, 103

COSMIC WIRE, 174

CRYSTAL CHILDREN, 149

DALAI LAMA, 124

DAMAGED CHAKRAS, 77

DIVINE RIGHT OF KINGS, 132

DIVINE WORLD ORDER, 185

DNA, 166, 167

DOLPHINS, 71

EDGE OF POSSIBILITY, 55

EDGE OF TIME, 14, 40, 55, 57, 58

ELDERS, 69

ELITES, 108, 110, 111, 114, 115, 116, 117, 119, 120, 121, 122, 123, 124, 126, 128, 129, 131, 133, 134, 136, 137, 139, 142, 145, 171

EMISSARIES, 115

EMOTIONAL COLOR, 88

EMOTIONS, 29, 88, 95, 101, 108, 159, 169

EMPIRICISM, 130

EMPIRICISM, 130

ENERGY, 19, 21, 63, 70, 86, 88, 94, 172

ENERGY, 21

ENERGY GAMBIT, 115

ENERGY OF CREATION, 24, 33, 35, 61, 62, 63, 73, 74, 77, 79, 86, 87, 88, 181

ENERGY WORKER, 15

ENSLAVEMENT, 104

EVOLUTION, 11, 26, 63, 67, 80, 101, 102, 103

FAMILY OF SPIRIT, 70

FEAR, 30, 37, 68, 69, 76, 82, 99, 107, 108, 109, 110, 116, 126, 134, 143, 150, 153, 155, 158, 160, 161, 164, 165, 166, 167, 169, 170, 171, 172, 173, 179, 184, 185

FEARS, 30, 145, 155, 164, 165, 166, 167, 168, 169, 170, 177, 178, 184, 185

FISH BOWL, 38

GOLDEN RULE, 92

GOOD NEWS, 12, 82, 114, 154, 156

GRAYS, 101, 104, 105, 106, 107, 108, 109, 111

GUIDE NETWORK, 96, 97, 98, 124, 125

GUIDES, 45, 96, 97, 99, 124, 125, 127, 129, 153, 155, 156, 157, 159, 160, 172, 173, 174, 184

HEALERS, 142

HOLY SPIRIT, 174

IMMORTAL SPIRIT, 14, 21, 23, 26, 32, 41, 42, 43, 44, 46, 51, 55, 58, 59, 60, 63, 64, 65, 66, 68, 71, 72, 73, 81, 83, 89, 90, 91, 99, 102, 103, 114, 116, 117, 140, 181

INDIGO CHILDREN, 149

INFORMATION COMMONS, 137

INFRASTRUCTURE OF LIGHT, 118, 120, 121, 127, 128, 129, 132

INTENT, 14, 21, 22, 23, 24, 28, 29, 31, 33, 36, 37, 38, 42, 44, 45, 46, 49, 50, 51, 59, 61, 63, 64, 67, 70, 74, 78, 79, 80, 82, 86, 87, 92, 93, 98, 103, 118, 120, 156, 163, 175, 176, 182

JUDGMENT, 30, 93

KARMA, 86, 96, 97, 98, 149, 156, 157, 158, 160, 161, 162, 174, 176, 177, 179

KARMIC CONTRACT, 96, 97

KUNDALINI, 171, 174, 175, 176

LADDER OF CREATION, 12, 66, 85

LAW OF SPIRITUAL RESPONSIBILITY, 91

LAWS OF PHYSICALITY, 39

LEMURIA, 62, 66, 67, 69, 70, 80, 81, 83, 85

LEMURIAN, 67, 68, 69, 70, 80, 81, 83

LIGHT BODY, 78, 108, 119

MANIFESTATION, 21, 34, 46, 47, 48, 49, 64, 71, 73, 77, 86,

87, 88, 90, 92, 96, 97, 101, 104, 107, 126, 145, 167, 178
MANIFESTATION DEVICE, 72
MATRIX, 61, 152, 179
MAYAN, 67
MAYANS, 55, 56
MERKABA, 76, 78, 79, 80, 108, 154
MOMENT, 33, 43, 46, 47, 48, 49, 50, 51, 52, 54, 56, 58, 60, 92, 117, 122, 179
MONAD, 53, 54, 72, 154, 159
MOTHER NATURE, 87
NEUTRALITY, 86, 87, 88
NUTRITION, 134, 142, 176
OLD WORLD, 56, 180, 181, 184
ONE LAW OF THE UNIVERSE, 91
ORIGINAL SPIN, 88, 90
OUROBOROS, 48, 49
PAST LIFE, 51
PERSISTENCE, 86, 87, 88
PHYSICALITY, 14, 23, 28, 29, 32, 34, 35, 36, 37, 38, 40, 43, 44, 45, 46, 47, 50, 53, 55, 60, 63, 64, 66, 67, 71, 73, 74, 77, 78, 80, 81, 82, 85, 91, 95, 96, 98, 99, 114, 119, 141, 144, 154, 159
POLARITIES OF CREATION, 33
PRINTING TECHNOLOGY, 136
PROBABILISTIC PROPHECY, 57
PROCESSED FOODS, 72, 176
PURVEYORS OF TRUTH, 145
QUALITATIVE IMPRINT, 87
QUANTUM BOUNDARY, 32, 36, 81, 83
RESPONSIVENESS OF ENERGY, 92
RETRIBUTION, 93, 94
ROY G BIV, 74
RULE BY GOVERNMENT, 132

SCARCITY, 70, 103
SHAMBHALA, 12, 29, 145
SLAVE MASTERS, 109, 113
SLAVERY, 68, 69, 104, 105, 113, 115, 116
SOCIAL DARWINISM, 134
SPACE/TIME TUBE, 41, 43, 46, 49, 52, 55, 57, 58, 60, 62, 73, 91, 95, 111, 114, 140, 142, 143, 144
SPARKS OF THE ONE, 32, 70, 160, 173, 183
SPIRIT, 24, 27, 28, 29, 42, 43, 44, 46, 49, 50, 51, 55, 58, 59, 60, 69, 71, 72, 73, 74, 76, 81, 82, 83, 85, 87, 89, 92, 101, 105, 107, 114, 115, 116, 117, 118, 119, 122, 127, 130, 143, 145, 153, 160, 164, 167, 169, 172, 173, 183
SPIRITUAL MASTER, 119
STAR OF DAVID, 78
STARSEED, 59, 60, 114, 118, 120, 132, 136, 137, 140, 141, 150, 179, 184
STARSEEDS, 56, 59, 120, 122, 124, 128, 129, 130, 131, 132, 136, 141, 142, 143, 144
SYMPATHETIC VIBRATION, 88, 89, 94
THE ASCENSION, 12, 13, 14, 15, 19, 20, 21, 30, 31, 35, 36, 37, 38, 48, 56, 59, 61, 62, 63, 64, 66, 67, 70, 81, 83, 112, 113, 115, 179
THE ONE LAW, 91, 94
THE PATH
THE PATH, 50, 95, 122, 124, 130, 143, 156, 171, 179, 180, 183
THE VEIL, 52, 54, 89

THREE DAYS OF DARKNESS, 185

TIME, 37, 38, 39, 40, 43, 52, 55

TRANSMUTING ENERGY, 94, 96, 162

TREE OF LIFE. SEE LADDER OF CREATION.

UNIVERSAL SPIRITUAL LAW, 91

VALENCE, 86, 87, 88, 89, 90, 96, 97, 99

VISIONARY PROPHECY, 57

WAR OF SOULS, 114, 117, 120, 127, 128, 145, 150

WARRIORS, 143, 144

WEB OF LIGHT, 137

WORLD ELITES, 114, 115, 116, 117, 119, 121, 127, 171, 180

WORLD WIDE WEB WWW, 137, 139, 140

YANG, 32, 33, 34, 35, 61, 63, 64, 65, 66, 70, 71, 72, 77, 78, 79, 80, 81, 83, 87, 89, 99, 173, 181, 182

YIN, 32, 33, 34, 35, 61, 63, 64, 65, 66, 68, 71, 78, 79, 80, 81, 82, 87, 99, 124, 153, 173, 181, 182, 184

A GIFT FROM AVATAR
THE SONG OF CREATION FREE!

I just finished THE BOOK OF LIFE, DOSSIER OF THE ASCENSION, and THE SONG OF CREATION. What an extraordinary contribution you've made to the enlightenment of our little species! These are the best spiritual books I've read since Yogananda's commentary on the Gita.
William T. Hathaway author of Summer Snow, and winner of a Rinehart Foundation Award.

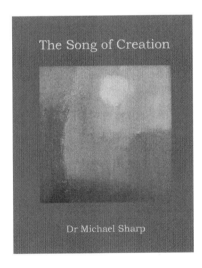

The Song of Creation is Michael Sharp's fourth book.

The Song of Creation is the complete and canonical story of creation. From "the beginning" to the ascension of this universe, our collective path, and your role in it.

The Song of Creation provides a powerful cadence to the previous work of Michael Sharp and is a testament to the power of Michael Sharp's pen.

Read the full text now as a beautifully illustrated PDF document! http://www.michaelsharp.org/genesis/

The illustrated *Song of Creation* (ISBN 0-9737401-6-7) is also available for you to share with family and friends as a full color book. It is available from Amazon.com and its international derivatives, Barnes and Noble, your local retailer, and wherever fine books are sold. Distributed by Ingram, Baker and Taylor, New Leaf and others.

DOSSIER OF THE ASCENSION
A PRACTICAL GUIDE TO CHAKRA ACTIVATION
AND KUNDALINI AWAKENING

ISBN: 0-9735379-3-0
http://www.avatarpublication.com/

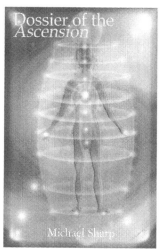

A book with a message of power.

Learn how to activate your chakras and stay activated. Learn what to expect as you move from inefficient co-creator to powerful co-creator of the physical universe around you. Learn how easy it is to overcome blockage and attain the holy grail of Spiritual attainment – *full chakra activation and safe kundalini activation.*

With the skill that only a master can bring, Michael Sharp provides all the guidance you need in order to shrug off the chains that keep you away from your spiritual power and birthright. With *The Dossier* in hand, you will quickly and efficiently throw off the fears and misconceptions that keep your chakras blocked and your kundalini in bondage.

The Dossier is a must read for anybody serious about spiritual empowerment or ascension.

The Dossier of the Ascension is available directly from Avatar Publications, Amazon.com and its international derivatives, Barnes and Noble, your local retailer, and wherever fine books are sold. Distributed by Ingram, Baker and Taylor, New Leaf, and others.

THE BOOK OF LIGHT: THE NATURE OF GOD, THE STRUCTURE OF CONSCIOUSNESS, AND THE UNIVRSEWITHIN YOU

ISBN: 0-9738555-2-5

http://www.avatarpublication.com

The Book of Light is probably the best Kabbalahist description of the creation of consciousness that I have ever read.
Tami Brady – Midwest Review of Books

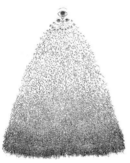

The Book of Light

The Nature of God, the Structure of Consciousness and the Universe Within You

Volume One
by Dr Michael Sharp

When you are ready to remove your chains.

The Book of Light is a spiritual tour-de-force that will take you on a journey of enlightenment and empowerment like no other. Expressing only the highest spiritual truths, yet written in the same down-to-earth manner as all Michael Sharp's books, The Book of Light will leave you breathless and at the edge of your seat wanting more from this remarkable spiritual teacher. It is a gift of total freedom from the bondage of the veil. *The Book of Light* will help you place yourself in proper perspective not as a descended ape or fallen angel but as the glorious, light filled spark of divine creator conscious that you are. It will remove the final vestiges of sleep and give you back your full and limitless potential. Haven't you put up with all the nonsense long enough? It is time to return. Welcome Home!

The Book of Light is available directly from Avatar Publications, Amazon.com and its international derivatives, Barnes and Noble, your local retailer, and wherever fine books are sold. Distributed by Ingram, Baker and Taylor, New Leaf, and others

AWAKENING:
HOW EXTRATERRESTRIAL CONTACT
CAN TRANSFORM YOUR LIFE

ISBN: 0-9738442-0-5

http://www.avatarpublication.com

The new bible of the "abductee" phenomenon.

Up until now the phenomena of alien abduction has been presented in a bleak, oppressive, threatening, and fear filled fashion. As we all "know", abductees are victims and counselors help them cope.

But what if it is not like that at all? What if it is only our fear that makes us see this way and prevents us from seeing the truth? What if alien "abductions" are not about experimentation and probing but about spiritual awakening and galactic contact?

Sound fantastic? This is just what Mary Rodwell, counselor, registered nurse, and midwife, suggests in Awakenings. After working with over 900 experiencers (a.k.a. abductees) Mary concludes that it is our fear that prevents us from seeing the truth and our fear that creates our terror. Once we overcome fear we see the phenomenon for what it really is.

It is past time that we shrugged off our fear of this amazing spiritual phenomenon. Let Mary help you overcome the fear and conditioning that prevents you from seeing the profound and beautiful truth.

There are ships on our horizon!

Awakening is available directly from Avatar Publications, Amazon.com and its international derivatives, Barnes and Noble, your local retailer, and wherever fine books are sold. Distributed by Ingram, Baker and Taylor, New Leaf, and others.

SUMMER SNOW

ISBN: 0-9738442-3-X
http://www.avatarpublication.com

SUMMER SNOW is a spiritual novel set now amidst the war on terrorism as an American warrior falls in love with a Sufi mystic and learns from her an alternative to the military mentality.

As US Special Forces battle al-Qaeda, the escalating violence threatens their future together and the lives of thousands in her country. To save them, she shows him an ancient transcendental way to bring peace to the collective consciousness and prevent terrorism. But can they make it work in time?

A story of love in the shadow of destruction, SUMMER SNOW blends passion, adventure, and mystic wisdom to convey its theme that higher consciousness is more effective than violence and that women may be more able than men to lead us there.

> Hathaway skillfully weaves a touching love story into this modern day adventure thriller. Sufi mystics, militant terrorists, and atavistic men of every nationality come together in surprising ways. SUMMER SNOW is a true picture of the world we live in as it is, and as it could be if lasting love and peace were possible. William Hathaway's exceptional writing style makes this novel a stand out".

Laurel Johnson – Midwest Book Review

3492958

Made in the USA